For Susan

50

great appetizers

Buon appetito !

By Pamela Sheldon Johns

Produced by Jennifer Barry Designs

Photographs by Joyce Oudkerk Pool

Pamela Sheldon Johns

Andrews McMeel
Publishing, LLC
Kansas City

Concept and Design: Jennifer Barry Design, Fairfax, California
Production Assistance: Kristen Hall
Food Styling: Pouké

08 09 10 11 12 TWP 10 9 8 7 6 5 4 3 2 1

ISBN-13: 978-0-7407-7650-2
ISBN-10: 0-7407-7650-9

Library of Congress Cataloging-in-Publication data is on file.

www.andrewsmcmeel.com

Attention: Schools and Businesses

Andrews McMeel books are available at quantity discounts with bulk purchase for
educational, business, or sales promotional use. For information, please write to:
Special Sales Department, Andrews McMeel Publishing, LLC, 1130 Walnut Street,
Kansas City, Missouri 64106.

great appetizers 5

topped & dipped 11

grilled & skewered 37

stuffed & rolled 55

plated & sauced 85

basics 104
equivalents 106
acknowledgments 107
sources 108
index 109

great appetizers

Everyone loves tasting lots of different little things! My favorite party to give or to go to is an appetizer party. Starters, amuses-bouche, antipasti, hors d'oeuvres, mezes, antojitos, dim sum, tapas, canapés, finger foods—no matter what you call them, almost every culture has some kind of appetizer. By definition, an appetizer is a food served before a meal to stimulate the appetite. These little tidbits of food literally get the juices flowing and signal that there may be more to come.

I am about to give you my best entertaining secret. It is the one that causes everyone to walk into my house with their mouth watering and the thought that Pamela is a great cook: No matter what I am serving, just before my guests arrive, I cook something that will fill the house with tantalizing food scents. Usually, I sauté some onions or garlic, an irresistible aroma for the already hungry. In the holiday season, I caramelize a little sugar or drip some vanilla on a hot nonstick pan or simmer apple juice with cinnamon sticks in it. In the summer, I put hickory chips and one hamburger patty on the grill and fill the

air with savory essences that would make a vegetarian crave meat. I am shameless when it comes to feeding people and exceedingly satisfied when they ask for seconds.

Party Planning

Start your planning with the invitations, and be sure to request an RSVP so that you will have a somewhat accurate count of the number of guests. Decide on your theme and what type of party you will have. Appetizers can be the main event of a party, the teasers before a meal, or the first course of a sit-down repast. In planning your menu for any of these possibilities, you should choose a range of recipes with a good diversity of ingredients, colors, temperatures, levels of spiciness, and textures.

The more variety, the more interesting the table is, but you can make yourself crazy if you try to do too many things. Supplement the assorted platters with baskets of breads, chips, and bowls of nuts. A cheese tray is an easy way to fill out a table; an assortment of Cheddar, smoked provolone, blue cheese, a wedge of Brie, and a basket of sliced breads is always popular. Have a supply of back-up goodies in your pantry in case you come up short: olives, tapenade, pickles, crackers, and salsas are foods that won't spoil if you don't use them and will keep your party from being spoiled if you need them.

Take into consideration any guests with unique needs, such as children. It's fun to make a special little table just for the kids, with tea sandwiches, fruit, crackers, and cheese. Don't forget about the vegetarians; a beautifully displayed platter of crudités will please everyone. If you are expecting several vegetarians, provide a separate table with just vegetable dishes that they and everyone else can choose from.

Once your menu is planned, determine which dishes can be made ahead and what needs to be cooked or assembled at the last moment. Don't try to do all of your recipes at the last minute; have some dishes already prepared so that you're not rushing at the last minute. For example, most dipping sauces and marinated foods can be prepared a day before.

With your timeline in place, you can make your shopping lists. To calculate quantities for a party, the rule of thumb is 8 to 10 portions per person for an appetizers-only party. If a meal is to follow, reduce these portions by half.

At least a week before the party, ask yourself a few questions: Will you need to rent dishes, glasses, eating utensils, tables, linens, chairs, chafing dishes, and serving utensils? Do you have enough refrigeration? Will you use disposable eating utensils? Will you need staffing to help park cars, cook, serve, and/or clean up? Is weather a concern, and do you have an option if it rains? Yes, that's a lot of questions, but it's better to think of these things in advance.

Party Perfect!

Presentation is very important. Consider using edible garnishes, such as olives, cheeses, bread sticks, grapes, figs, strawberries, and tangerine slices. Display appetizers on beds of lettuce leaves, edible flowers, or sliced citrus or tomato. Instead of traditional trays, make use of handsome wooden cutting boards, slabs of marble, and decorative mirrors. Give your table several layers of height by using cake stands, small boxes draped with linens, and floral arrangements. If you have a number of different sauces and dips, make name tags describing what they are.

Set up a beverage station; self-service is the easiest, but it still needs to be monitored to keep clean glasses, ice, and plenty of drinks available, including water and nonalcoholic beverages. Music, live or recorded, gives a party its tone.

Once you have your serving tables set up, have extra serving platters already assembled in the kitchen to exchange for empties when needed. It's usually easier to keep the hot and cold foods in separate serving areas to make it easier to replenish.

Food Safety

Please remember food safety: food should remain at room temperature for a maximum of 2 hours, or 1 hour at the most on a hot day. Be aware of what ingredients are in your dishes, even those you have purchased, in case there are people with allergies or special diets.

Getting Started: Party Menus and Themes

Most of the following recipes serve 8 people (with 2 or 3 portions per person) and can be easily doubled or tripled. Here are some thematic menus, along with serving and decorating suggestions.

Mexican

Papaya-Avocado Salsa with Quesadilla Triangles

Tortilla Rolls with Corn & Black Bean Salsa

Lemon Chicken Escabeche

Roasted Poblano Chilies Stuffed with Shrimp
& Crab

Add a basket of chips, some fresh tomato salsa, and guacamole. Garnish the platters with sprinkles of diced jicama, corn kernels, and diced red bell peppers. Suggested beverages: Mexican beer, margaritas, and sangría.

Italian

Antipasto platter: White Bean–Rosemary Crostini, Heirloom Tomato Bruschetta, Chicken Liver Crostini

Mozzarella, Basil, & Cherry Tomato Skewers

Bite-Sized Polenta Squares with Goat Cheese & Sun-Dried Tomatoes

Prosciutto & Arugula Mini Pizzas

The red-checkered tablecloth and straw-wrapped Chianti bottles are corny, but cute. Add a cutting board spread with a variety of *salumi* and Italian cheeses. Serve Prosecco, Pinot Grigio, and a good Italian red wine.

Farmers' Market (Vegetarian)

Heirloom Tomato Bruschetta

Herbed Goat Cheese Dip with Crudité

Grilled Baby Vegetables

Stuffed Zucchini Blossoms

Four-Seasons Frittata

Create baskets or platters of fresh fruits and vegetables for display. Drinks should include smoothies, fresh-squeezed juices, and wine coolers.

Pacific Rim

Fried Spring Rolls with Peanut Dipping Sauce

Vegetable Samosas

Tea-Smoked Chicken Wings

Orange-Broccoli Salad

Instead of serving spoons and forks, use chopsticks. Decorate the platters with snow peas, baby corn, and baby carrots. Have bowls of steamed edamame and Asian party mix (rice crackers and wasabi peas) on the side. Paper lanterns can embellish the décor.

Mediterranean

Baba Ghanoush with Toasted Pita Triangles

Stuffed Grape Leaves with Dilled Yogurt

B'Stilla

Provençal Tomato-Basil Tartlets

Use fresh grape or fig leaves to line platters and sprinkle the rims with pomegranate seeds. Decorate with large bunches of red grapes. Serve white and red wine and sparkling water with lemon slices.

All Seafood

Scallops with Cilantro–Pine Nut Dipping Sauce

Champagne Oysters

Pepper-Crusted Tuna, Onion, & Bell Pepper Skewers

Grilled Scallops Wrapped in Pancetta

Mini Salmon Cakes

Marinated Mussels & Clams

Classic wine wisdom says to serve white wines with seafood, but a nice rosé or light red will also work with most of these dishes.

Island Party

Papaya-Avocado Salsa with Quesadilla Triangles

Grilled Fresh Fruit

Skewered Hawaiian Sweet & Sour Meatballs

Pepper-Crusted Tuna, Onion, & Bell Pepper Skewers

Leis for each guest! Instead of serving on trays, use banana leaves. For the table, palm fronds, whole coconuts, and lots of flowers such as hibiscuses and birds-of-paradise. Essential beverages include Piña Coladas, Mai Tais, and fruit punch.

'50s Cocktail Party

Grilled Shrimp Skewers

Skewered Hawaiian Sweet & Sour Meatballs

Grilled Lemon Chicken Wings

Grilled Scallops Wrapped in Pancetta

Stuffed Baby Potatoes with Mushroom Puree &
Creme Fraîche

Deviled Quail Eggs with Capers & Flying Fish Caviar

This feels like a retro pool party, so serve martinis,
of course, preferably from a bar. Campy platters of
cheese cubes with frilly toothpicks are appropriate.
Pull out your poodle skirt and the turntable with those
old Sinatra and Nat King Cole vinyls.

Vegetarian

Below is a list of the recipes included in this book that
contain no meat, seafood, or poultry. Some may call
for chicken stock, but this can easily be substituted
with vegetable stock (page 105):

Baba Ghanoush with Toasted Pita Triangles

White Bean–Rosemary Crostini

Pesto Dip with Spicy Bread Twists

Heirloom Tomato Bruschetta

Herbed Goat Cheese Dip with Crudité

Baby Artichokes with Red Pepper Mayonnaise

Papaya-Avocado Salsa with Quesadilla Triangles

Bite-Sized Polenta Squares with Goat Cheese
& Sun-Dried Tomatoes

Potato–Red Onion Flat Bread

Provençal Tomato-Basil Tartlets

Mozzarella, Basil, & Cherry Tomato Skewers

Grilled Baby Vegetables

Grilled Fresh Fruit

Grilled Portobello Mushrooms with Crumbled Stilton

Grilled Eggplant Rolls Stuffed with Herbed Ricotta

Fried Spring Rolls with Peanut Dipping Sauce

Stuffed Grape Leaves with Dilled Yogurt

Tortilla Rolls with Corn & Black Bean Salsa

Crispy Parmigiano Shells Stuffed with Mixed
Greens

Vegetable Samosas

Stuffed Cabbage Rolls

Stuffed Baby Potatoes with Mushroom Puree &
Creme Fraîche

Stuffed Zucchini Blossoms

Stuffed Tomatoes

Rice Croquettes Filled with Gorgonzola

Baked Brie with Apricots

Roasted Garlic & Leek Soufflé

Orange-Broccoli Salad

Marinated Mushrooms

Italian Ruby Chard Custard

topped & dipped

It is important to be flexible when planning your menu. Don't feel bound by the exact ingredients you see in the recipes that follow. Perhaps you will find an olive bread at the bakery or some interesting crackers to try with the toppings instead of the breads suggested here. Why not set out several toppings and several dips and let your guests build their own from baskets of bread, crackers, crudités, and chips? Almost all of the recipes in this section are do-ahead, which will leave you time to mingle and socialize. Just have plenty of food in the kitchen to replenish the platters, baskets, and bowls, and enjoy your party!

white bean-rosemary crostini

Crostini are a classic Tuscan appetizer. These can also be made with 2 cups of canned cannellini beans seasoned with some fresh herbs.

1 cup dried cannellini beans, rinsed
   and picked over

2 cloves garlic, peeled

1 sprig rosemary

3 tablespoons olive oil

½ onion, finely chopped

½ carrot, peeled and finely chopped

½ stalk celery, finely chopped

8 cups chicken stock (page 104)

1 tablespoon minced fresh flat-leaf
   parsley

Salt and freshly ground pepper

1 tablespoon chopped fresh rosemary
   for garnish

1 baguette, sliced

• Soak the beans overnight in water to cover, with the garlic and rosemary. The next day, drain the beans, reserving the garlic and rosemary.

• Heat the olive oil in a large, heavy saucepan over medium heat and sauté the onion, carrot, and celery until golden brown, 6 to 8 minutes.

• Add the chicken stock, drained beans, and the reserved garlic and rosemary. Bring to a boil, then lower the heat to a simmer. Add the parsley and cook, uncovered, until the beans are tender, 2½ to 3 hours. Drain the beans, reserving the cooking liquid. Puree the beans in a blender, adding some of the reserved cooking liquid as needed to keep the puree smooth, but not too thin to spread on the bread. Season with salt and pepper to taste.

• Spread the puree on the sliced bread, sprinkle with rosemary, and serve at once. *Serves 8*

pesto dip
with spicy bread twists

Pesto sauce is a great ingredient to have on hand to flavor everything from soups to dips. It can be made up to a week ahead of time; just float a layer of olive oil on top, cover, and refrigerate.

pesto dip

3 cloves garlic, peeled

1 bunch basil, stemmed

¼ cup pine nuts, toasted (see page 105)

½ cup extra-virgin olive oil

¼ cup grated Parmigiano-Reggiano cheese

spicy bread twists

1 sheet frozen puff pastry, thawed

¾ cup (3 ounces) grated Parmigiano-Reggiano cheese

1 tablespoon freshly ground pepper

1 teaspoon dried oregano

½ teaspoon salt

2 large eggs, lightly beaten

Cayenne pepper for dusting

• To make the pesto: Drop the garlic into a food processor with the machine running. Add the basil and pine nuts and process to a grainy texture. With the machine running, gradually add the olive oil to the desired consistency. Fold in the cheese by hand. *Makes 1 cup*

• To make the bread twists: Place the puff pastry sheet on a lightly floured work surface. With a sharp knife, cut it crosswise into twenty-four ¼-inch-wide strips. Fold each strip in half lengthwise and roll into a 10-inch-long strip.

• Combine the cheese, pepper, oregano, and salt in a shallow dish; stir with a whisk to blend. Put the eggs in another shallow dish. Dip each puff pastry strip into the egg, then dredge in the cheese mixture. Set aside on the floured work surface until all of the strips are coated.

• Preheat the oven to 425°F. Oil a baking sheet or line it with parchment paper.

• Put the ends of 3 strips together and pinch tightly. Braid, then pinch the other end to secure. Place each braid on the prepared pan and refrigerate for 20 to 30 minutes.

• Lightly dust the twists with cayenne pepper. Bake the twists until golden brown, 8 to 10 minutes. Remove from the oven and let cool on a wire rack. Arrange on a platter and serve with the pesto dip alongside. *Serves 8*

heirloom tomato bruschetta

Exploit summer's best colors and flavors by using heirloom tomatoes. Include this appetizer on a vegetarian table along with Vegetable Samosas (page 64), and Provençal Tomato-Basil Tartlets (page 70).

6 ounces assorted heirloom tomatoes, diced

2 tablespoons extra-virgin olive oil, plus more for drizzling

5 leaves fresh basil, cut into fine shreds

Salt and freshly ground pepper

1 loaf country bread, sliced ½ inch thick

4 cloves garlic, peeled

• In a bowl, combine the tomatoes, the 2 tablespoons olive oil, and the basil. Season with salt and pepper to taste. Set aside.

• Grill or toast the bread slices on both sides. Remove from the heat and rub immediately with the garlic. Place on a serving platter, top with the tomato mixture, and drizzle with olive oil. *Serves 8*

chicken liver crostini
with apple slices

In Tuscany, where this dish was born, vin santo, a sweet wine, is sometimes used to deglaze the pan. Another delicious variation is to use balsamic vinegar instead of red wine vinegar.

1 tablespoon unsalted butter

2 tablespoons olive oil

2 tablespoons finely chopped pancetta

1/2 onion, finely chopped

8 ounces chicken livers

1/4 cup dry white wine

2 tablespoons red wine vinegar

1/2 teaspoon minced fresh thyme

1 tablespoon minced fresh flat-leaf parsley, plus 16 leaves for garnish

Salt and freshly ground pepper

1 baguette, sliced

1 Red Delicious apple, cored

• Melt the butter with the olive oil in a medium sauté pan over medium heat. Add the pancetta and onion and sauté until golden, 5 minutes. Add the chicken livers and wine; cook until the livers are firm, 12 to 15 minutes. Add the vinegar and stir to scrape up the browned bits from the bottom of the pan. Transfer the mixture to a food processor and process until smooth. Stir in the thyme, minced parsley, and salt and pepper to taste.

• Just before serving, spread chicken liver mixture on the bread slices. Cut the apple into thin slices and place 1 parsley leaf and a 1 apple slice on top of each bread slice. Arrange on a platter and serve at room temperature. *Serves 8*

baba ghanoush
with toasted pita triangles

This savory eggplant dip can also be used as a sandwich spread and is best made a day ahead. Serve it alongside other eggplant dishes, such as Grilled Eggplant Rolls (page 59) and Grilled Baby Vegetables (page 41).

2 large globe eggplants

Juice of 2 lemons

2 tablespoons tahini (sesame paste)

2 cloves garlic, minced

¼ teaspoon salt

Freshly ground white pepper

2 tablespoons minced fresh flat-leaf parsley

6 pita bread rounds, each cut into 4 wedges

Olive oil for brushing

• Preheat the oven to 400°F. Lightly oil a baking sheet.

• Cut the eggplants in half and place, cut side down, on the prepared pan. Roast for 40 minutes, or until dark and shriveled. Remove from the oven and let cool to the touch.

• Scoop out the pulp and place in a food processor or blender. Add the lemon juice, tahini, and garlic; process until smooth. Season with the salt and pepper to taste. Transfer to a serving bowl and sprinkle with the parsley.

• Place the pita wedges on a baking sheet, brush both sides lightly with olive oil, and toast in the oven for 5 minutes, turning halfway through the heating. Arrange on a tray with the bowl of baba ghanoush in the center. *Serves 8*

marinated mushrooms

A glass of sparkling Prosecco accompanies a platter of these mushrooms very well. For a variation, add some cured black olives. The flavors will marry better if the mushrooms are refrigerated overnight.

1 pound white mushrooms, stemmed

2 cloves garlic, minced

⅓ cup white wine vinegar

1 cup extra-virgin olive oil

Salt, freshly ground pepper, and
**   red pepper flakes**

2 tablespoons minced fresh flat-leaf
**   parsley**

• Cut the mushroom caps in half and put in a bowl. Combine the garlic and vinegar in a small bowl. Gradually whisk in the olive oil. Season with salt, pepper, and pepper flakes to taste. Pour over the mushrooms and let stand at room temperature for 1 hour, or refrigerate for at least 2 hours or as long as overnight. Drain the mushrooms and place on a serving platter. Sprinkle with the parsley and serve at room temperature. *Serves 8*

herbed goat cheese dip

A large tray of fresh vegetables appeals to young and old. Blanching vegetables preserves their vivid color. Place baskets of chips and other dips nearby so that guests can mix and match.

1 cup cauliflower florets

3 carrots, peeled and cut into
  4-inch sticks

1 cup broccoli florets

1 cup 4-inch pieces asparagus

1 small jicama, peeled and cut into
  4-inch sticks

2 red bell peppers, cut into 4-inch strips

6 ounces fresh goat cheese at room
  temperature

⅓ cup heavy cream

2 tablespoons minced fresh garlic
  chives

1 teaspoon minced fresh mint

Salt and freshly ground white pepper

• Prepare a pot of salted boiling water. In the following order, drop in the cauliflower, carrots, broccoli, and asparagus, in separate batches, cooking each one for about 30 seconds, then immersing the batch immediately in ice water to stop the cooking. Drain well and pat dry. Arrange the blanched vegetables, jicama, and peppers on a platter.

• Combine the goat cheese, cream, chives, and mint in a small bowl and stir to blend. Season with salt and pepper to taste. Place in a dipping bowl and serve alongside the crudités. *Serves 8*

baby artichokes
with red pepper mayonnaise

This elegant presentation can also be made with artichoke hearts if baby artichokes are not available. The red pepper mayonnaise is wonderful in almost any recipe that calls for mayonnaise, from potato salad to tea sandwiches.

red pepper mayonnaise

1 red bell pepper

2 large egg yolks at room temperature

2 tablespoons fresh lemon juice

2 tablespoons white wine vinegar

2 cups canola oil

1/2 teaspoon dry mustard

Salt and freshly ground white pepper

8 baby artichokes

1 lemon, halved

1/4 cup olive oil

1 cup finely chopped onion

3 cloves garlic, minced

2 carrots, peeled and diced

3/4 cup dry white wine

1/2 cup vegetable stock (page 105)

Bouquet garni: 1 parsley sprig,

1 thyme sprig, and 1 bay leaf,

tied in a cheesecloth square

1/4 teaspoon salt

Freshly ground pepper

• To make the red pepper mayonnaise: Place the red pepper directly on the stove top over a high gas flame, or on a baking sheet under a broiler as close to the heat source as possible. Turn the pepper frequently until blackened all over. Place it in a brown paper bag, close the bag, and let cool for about 15 minutes. Peel the pepper by scraping the blackened skin off with a sharp knife or your fingers. Remove the stem and seeds. Set aside.

• Combine the egg yolks, lemon juice, and vinegar in a blender. With the machine running, add the oil in very fine, steady stream. Add the roasted pepper and puree until smooth. Stir in salt and pepper to taste. *Makes 2½ cups*

• Trim the tops of the artichokes and remove the coarse outer leaves. Cut the base of 4 artichokes flat so they will stand upright. Cut the remaining artichokes in half lengthwise. Remove the fine center leaves and cut each artichoke in half lengthwise again to create quarters. Rub all cut surfaces with lemon.

• Heat the olive oil in a large, heavy skillet or Dutch oven over medium heat. Add the onion, garlic, and carrots and sauté until the onion is softened, about 3 minutes. Stir in the wine, increase the heat to high, and cook to reduce the liquid by one-third.

• Add the vegetable stock and return to a boil. Lower the heat to a simmer; add the bouquet garni, salt, pepper to taste, and the whole artichokes, standing them in the pan. Cover and cook for 20 minutes. Add the artichoke quarters and cook, stirring occasionally, until the artichokes are tender, 25 to 30 minutes longer. With tongs, arrange on a platter, drizzle with the mayonnaise, and serve. *Serves 8*

papaya-avocado salsa
with quesadilla triangles

Your guests will smile when holding a margarita in one hand and these quesadilla triangles in the other. This versatile salsa is also delicious with grilled meat skewers or a basket of tortilla chips.

1 papaya, peeled, seeded, and cubed

1 avocado, peeled, pitted, and diced

1 red onion, diced

1/2 red bell pepper, seeded, deribbed, and diced

2 cloves garlic, minced

3 tablespoons extra-virgin olive oil

Juice of 2 limes

Salt and freshly ground pepper

8 flour tortillas

1 1/2 cups (6 ounces) grated Asiago cheese

• Combine the papaya, avocado, onion, bell pepper, garlic, olive oil, and lime juice in a medium bowl. Season with salt and pepper to taste and toss lightly. Set aside.

• Heat a large nonstick skillet over medium heat. Lay 1 tortilla in the pan and add a generous sprinkle of cheese. Top with another tortilla and cook, turning once or twice, until the tortilla is crisp and cheese is melted, 3 to 4 minutes. Using a metal spatula, transfer the tortilla to a cutting board and cut into 4 triangles. Keep warm in a low oven while cooking the remaining quesadillas. Serve on a warmed platter, with the papaya-avocado salsa in the center or alongside. *Serves 8*

bite-sized polenta squares
with goat cheese & sun-dried tomatoes

For holiday parties, cut out the polenta with a theme-shaped cookie cutter, such as Christmas trees, or hearts for Valentine's Day.

2 tablespoons olive oil

¼ cup finely chopped onion

2¼ cups chicken stock (page 104)

¾ cup polenta

¼ cup chopped oil-packed sun-dried tomatoes

1 tablespoon minced fresh flat-leaf parsley

½ teaspoon minced fresh thyme

Salt and freshly ground pepper

2 ounces fresh goat cheese, cut into ½-inch dice

• Lightly oil an 8-inch square baking dish. Heat the 2 tablespoons oil in a large, heavy saucepan over medium heat. Add the onion and sauté until golden, about 5 minutes. Stir in the chicken stock and bring to a boil. Whisking constantly, gradually add the polenta to the stock in a fine stream. Lower the heat to medium and cook, stirring constantly, for 10 to 15 minutes, or until the polenta thickens and easily comes away from the sides of the pot.

• Stir in the chopped sun-dried tomatoes, parsley, and thyme and season with salt and pepper to taste. Pour into the prepared dish, smoothing the top with a rubber spatula. Set aside to cool completely.

• To serve, cut the polenta into 1-inch squares. Top each square with a small piece of goat cheese and serve. *Serves 8*

29

potato-red onion flat bread

This moist flat bread, or focaccia, can be topped with your choice of ingredients, such as sliced figs and crumbled Gorgonzola or seasonal vegetables. Flat bread is an excellent accompaniment to grilled meats and vegetables.

3 russet potatoes, peeled

1 package active dry yeast

2 teaspoons sugar

3½ to 4 cups all-purpose flour

1 teaspoon salt

Extra-virgin olive oil for brushing

1 red onion, cut into ¼-inch-thick slices

¾ cup (3 ounces) shredded
Parmigiano-Reggiano cheese

1 tablespoon coarse sea salt

2 tablespoons minced fresh sage

• Cut 2 of the potatoes into 1-inch chunks. Put in a medium saucepan, cover with water, and boil until tender, about 20 minutes. Drain, reserving the cooking water. Pass the potatoes through a ricer or food mill.

• Stir the yeast and sugar into ½ cup of the reserved warm (105° to 115°F) potato-cooking water until dissolved. Let stand for 5 minutes, or until foamy.

• In a heavy-duty mixer fitted with a dough hook (or by hand), mix the flour, riced potatoes, and salt together. Add the yeast mixture and ¾ cup of the remaining potato water and mix to make a soft dough, 2 to 3 minutes.

continued next page

potato-red onion flat bread
(continued)

• Transfer to a lightly floured work surface and knead until smooth and elastic, 3 to 4 minutes. Place in a lightly oiled bowl and turn to coat. Cover with plastic wrap or a damp cloth and let rise in a warm place until doubled, about 1 hour.

• Lightly oil a baking sheet. Roll the dough out on a lightly floured work surface to fit the baking sheet. Place the dough on the sheet, cover with a dry towel, and let rise until doubled, about 30 minutes.

• Preheat the oven to 425°F. Scrub the remaining potato and cut it into ¼-inch-thick slices. Blanch the potato slices in salted boiling water until softened but not falling apart, 2 to 3 minutes.

• Brush the foccacia with olive oil and press with your fingertips all over the surface to create "dimples." Top with the onion, potato slices, and cheese. Sprinkle with sea salt.

• Bake for 25 to 30 minutes until the edges are lightly browned and the cheese is melted. Remove from the oven and let cool. To serve, cut into 3-inch squares, garnish with the sage, and arrange on a platter. *Serves 8*

prosciutto & arugula mini pizzas

At a casual party, this is a fun way to let your guests participate. Prepare the dough ahead, then set out a choice of toppings and let them make their own pizzas.

1 package active dry yeast

12 tablespoons sugar

½ cups warm (105° to 115°F) water

3½ cups all-purpose flour

½ cup semolina

1 tablespoon salt

3 tablespoons olive oil

1 cup (4 ounces) shredded part-skim
   mozzarella cheese

2 ounces prosciutto, thinly sliced

2 cups arugula leaves

• Stir the yeast and sugar into the warm water until dissolved. Let stand until foamy, about 5 minutes.

• In a heavy-duty mixer fitted with a dough hook (or by hand), combine the flour, semolina, and salt. Add the yeast mixture and olive oil and mix to a smooth dough. On a lightly floured work surface, knead the dough until smooth and elastic, 10 to 12 minutes.

Shape into a ball, place in a lightly oiled bowl, and turn to coat. Cover with plastic wrap or a damp towel and let rise in a warm place for 30 minutes, or until doubled in volume.

• Punch the dough down and divide into 8 pieces. Form into balls and place on a lightly oiled pan; cover with a dry towel and let rise for 45 minutes.

• Preheat the oven to 450°F with a pizza stone inside, or lightly oil a baking sheet. Roll the dough into 6-inch rounds and sprinkle a little mozzarella cheese onto each one, leaving a ½-inch border.

• Transfer the rounds to the pizza stone or prepared pan and bake for 4 to 5 minutes, or until the edges are lightly browned and the cheese is melted. Remove from the oven and top with the prosciutto and a pinch of arugula. Cut into quarters, arrange on a platter, and serve at once. *Makes 8 small pizzas*

tea-smoked chicken wings
with sweet & sour dipping sauce

This method of smoking can also be used with small, firm pieces of fish. Serve with other Asian-style dishes, such as Fried Spring Rolls with Peanut Sauce (page 56) and Orange-Broccoli Salad (page 100).

sweet & sour dipping sauce

¼ **cup soy sauce**

¼ **cup rice vinegar**

1½ **teaspoons minced garlic**

¼ **cup sugar**

½ **teaspoon Asian sesame oil**

¼ **cup raw rice (any kind)**

¼ **cup packed brown sugar**

2 **tablespoons orange or tangerine peel**

¼ **cup black tea leaves**

1 **tablespoon star anise pods**

24 **chicken wings**

• To make the dipping sauce: Combine the soy sauce, rice vinegar, garlic, and sugar in a small bowl. Whisk until the sugar is dissolved, then stir in the sesame oil. *Makes about ½ cup*

• Improvise a smoker by lining a wok or soup pot with aluminum foil, leaving a 2-inch collar extending above the top. Put the rice, sugar, orange peel, tea, and star anise in the bottom of the pan and place a wire rack on top of the rice mixture.

• Arrange the chicken wings on the rack and crimp the foil closed over it. Cover and smoke over medium heat for 15 minutes. Remove the pan from the heat and let stand for 10 minutes. Open the foil and transfer the wings to a serving plate. Serve warm, accompanied with the dipping sauce. *Serves 8*

scallops
with cilantro-pine nut dipping sauce

*This interesting variation on the classic pesto
on page 14 substitutes cilantro for the basil.
The dipping sauce can also be blended into
sour cream for a delicious dip for chips.*

cilantro–pine nut dipping sauce

3 cloves garlic, peeled

**1 cup lightly packed fresh cilantro
   leaves**

**¼ cup pine nuts, toasted
   (see page 105)**

About ½ cup extra-virgin olive oil

**¼ cup finely grated pecorino romano
   cheese**

3 tablespoons extra-virgin olive oil

24 sea scallops, rinsed and patted dry

**Sea salt and freshly ground white
   pepper**

• For the sauce: Drop the garlic into a food
processor with the machine running. Add the
cilantro and pine nuts and process to a grainy
texture. With the machine running, gradually
add about ½ cup olive oil to achieve the desired
consistency. Fold in the cheese by hand. Set
aside.

• Heat the 3 tablespoons olive oil in a large, heavy
sauté pan over medium heat. Add the scallops and
sauté until firm and lightly golden, about 2 minutes
on each side. Season with salt and pepper to taste.

• Pool the dipping sauce on a serving platter.
Arrange the scallops on top. Spear each scallop
with a toothpick. Alternately, serve the scallops
individually in ceramic Chinese soup spoons
drizzled with sauce for a dramatic effect. Serve
at once. *Serves 8*

grilled & skewered

Skewers are a great way to serve small bites and grilled appetizers. It's fun to think of interesting items to skewer foods with instead of the standard metal or bamboo skewers. For foods that don't need to be cooked on the skewer, why not use a chopstick or lemongrass spear for Asian-themed dishes? For bite-sized servings, consider using cocktail forks or bamboo picks instead of toothpicks. If grilling meats and other dense foods, I prefer stainless-steel skewers because they can tolerate higher temperatures and conduct some heat to the center of the food, allowing more even cooking. For quicker-cooking or raw foods, bamboo, birchwood, or elegant black willow skewers are a lovely choice. They come in a variety of lengths and thicknesses. When grilling or broiling with wood skewers, make sure to soak them in water for at least 30 minutes first to keep them from burning. Wrapping the exposed tips with aluminum foil also prevents charring.

grilled shrimp skewers

For these skewers, look for study rosemary branches and strip the lower two-thirds of the leaves off. Traditional skewers can also be used, but the rosemary branches perfume the shrimp as it cooks. Use a metal skewer to pierce the shrimp first, making it easier to insert the rosemary branch.

16 rosemary branches, leaves stripped from bottom 3 inches

16 jumbo shrimp, shelled and deveined

¼ cup extra-virgin olive oil

Juice of 1 lemon

1 teaspoon finely minced lemon zest

2 teaspoons minced fresh thyme

2 cloves garlic, minced

Freshly ground pepper

8 lemon wedges for serving

• Thread each rosemary "skewer" with a shrimp. Place in a shallow dish.

• In a small bowl, combine the olive oil, lemon juice, lemon zest, thyme, and garlic. Mix well and pour over the shrimp. Let marinate for at least 1 hour at room temperature.

• Preheat a grill or broiler. Remove the skewers from the marinade and season the shrimp with pepper to taste; grill, turning frequently and brushing with the marinade, until the shrimp are pink, 3 to 4 minutes. Serve with lemon wedges. *Serves 8*

pepper-crusted tuna, onion, & bell pepper skewers

Any firm-fleshed fish will work in this recipe. You can prepare the skewers in advance and marinate them until you are ready to grill.

1 teaspoon extra-virgin olive oil

1 tablespoon fresh lemon juice

1 pound tuna steak, cut into

    1-inch cubes

1 teaspoon green peppercorns

1 teaspoon pink peppercorns

1 teaspoon black peppercorns

1 teaspoon white peppercorns

2 red onions, cut into wedges and

    separated into layers

2 yellow bell peppers, seeded,

    deribbed, and cut into 1-inch pieces

Salt

• Soak 16 bamboo skewers in water for 30 minutes.

• Combine the olive oil and lemon juice in a medium bowl and whisk to blend. Add the tuna and toss to coat evenly.

• Combine the peppercorns in a small bowl and stir to blend. Spread them on a sided baking sheet and crush with a heavy skillet. Place the peppercorn mixture into a bowl and add the moistened tuna, tossing and pressing lightly to coat on all sides.

• Preheat a grill or broiler. Thread the tuna onto the skewers, alternating with the onion layers and bell pepper squares. Season with salt to taste and grill, turning occasionally, until the tuna is firm to the touch, about 5 minutes. *Serves 8*

grilled baby vegetables

Use seasonal vegetables for maximum flavor. For additional color, cherry tomatoes can be added during the last 2 minutes of cooking. These are also delicious served with Peanut Sauce (page 56) or Dilled Yogurt (page 62).

8 baby zucchini, stemmed

8 baby summer squash, stemmed

8 cipollini onions

8 white or cremini mushrooms,
**   cleaned and stemmed**

4 baby eggplants, halved lengthwise

16 cloves garlic, peeled

Olive oil for brushing

Salt and freshly ground pepper

• Soak 8 bamboo skewers in water for 30 minutes.

• Bring a pot of salted water to a boil. Drop in the zucchini and summer squash in separate batches, cooking each one for about 45 seconds, then immersing immediately in iced water to stop the cooking. Drain well and pat dry.

• Preheat a grill or broiler. Alternately thread an onion, zucchini, squash, mushroom, eggplant half, and 2 garlic cloves on each skewer. Brush the vegetables lightly with olive oil, season with salt and pepper to taste, and grill, turning frequently, until lightly browned, about 10 minutes. Transfer the skewers to a platter and serve at once. *Serves 8*

grilled fresh fruit

For sweet and savory sensation, red onion wedges are a nice addition to these skewers as well. Serve with grilled meats or seafood, such as Grilled Shrimp Skewers (page 38) or Grilled Scallops Wrapped in Pancetta (page 51).

**1 firm, ripe mango, peeled and cut
from the pit into chunks**

**1 firm, ripe papaya, peeled, seeded,
and cut into chunks**

**1 firm, ripe banana, peeled and cut
into chunks**

**¹⁄₂ pineapple, peeled, cored, and
cut into chunks**

Grated zest and juice of 4 limes

2 tablespoons brown sugar

A few drops of chili oil

Salt

• Soak 24 bamboo skewers in water for 30 minutes.

• Thread a piece of each type of fruit onto each skewer. Place in a shallow bowl and set aside.

• Combine the lime zest and juice, brown sugar, and chili oil in a small bowl and whisk until the sugar is dissolved. Pour over the fruit and let stand for 15 to 30 minutes.

• Preheat a grill or broiler. Sprinkle the fruit lightly with salt and grill, basting with the marinade and turning frequently, until lightly browned, 3 to 5 minutes. Place on a serving platter and drizzle with a little of the marinade to serve. *Serves 8*

mozzarella, basil, & cherry tomato skewers

This is the perfect summer appetizer— colorful, refreshing, and so easy! Have the kids help assemble the skewers, but watch out that they don't eat all of the ingredients!

6 ounces bocconcini (bite-sized mozzarella balls), drained well

1 pint cherry tomatoes (yellow and red)

Extra-virgin olive oil for drizzling

Salt and freshly ground pepper

6 leaves fresh basil, cut into fine shreds

• Thread the bocconcini onto 16 wooden skewers, alternating with the cherry tomatoes. Place on a platter, drizzle with olive oil, season with salt and pepper to taste, and sprinkle with the basil. *Serves 8*

skewered hawaiian sweet & sour meatballs

This appetizer reminds me of a dish my mother used to make! A little bit retro, it's perfect for a casual party. You can cook the meatballs ahead of time and reheat them in the oven.

½ cup all-purpose flour

1½ pounds ground veal

½ cup dried bread crumbs

1 small onion, finely chopped

2 cloves garlic, minced

2 large egg yolks

1 teaspoon grated fresh ginger

1 teaspoon salt

¼ cup pineapple juice

3 tablespoons extra-virgin olive oil

1 red bell pepper, seeded, deribbed, and cut into chunks

½ fresh pineapple, cored and cut into chunks

sauce

1 cup pineapple juice

¼ cup rice vinegar

1 tablespoon soy sauce

½ cup packed brown sugar

1 tablespoon cornstarch

• Put the flour in a shallow bowl. In a medium bowl, mix the ground veal, bread crumbs, onion, garlic, egg yolks, ginger, salt, and the ¼ cup pineapple juice. Form heaping tablespoons of the mixture firmly into 1-inch balls. Lightly roll the meatballs in the flour, shake them to remove the excess flour, then place them on a baking sheet or piece of parchment paper.

• Heat the oil in a large sauté pan over medium-high heat. Add the meatballs and cook, turning frequently, until browned on all sides, 4 to 5 minutes. Using a slotted spoon, transfer the meatballs to paper towels to drain. When cool enough to handle, thread each meatball onto a toothpick with 1 chunk bell pepper and 1 pineapple chunk. Arrange on a platter.

• For the sauce: Combine ¾ cup of the pineapple juice, the vinegar, and soy sauce in a small saucepan. Heat over medium heat, then add the brown sugar and stir until dissolved.

• Blend the cornstarch with the remaining ¼ cup pineapple juice in a small bowl and whisk into the saucepan. Cook, stirring constantly, until the mixture thickens slightly, 2 to 3 minutes. Pour into a small serving bowl and serve alongside the meatballs for dipping. *Serves 8*

grilled lemon chicken wings

Use a grilling basket to easily turn the chicken wings from one side to the other.

2 teaspoons grated lemon zest

½ cup fresh lemon juice

½ cup extra-virgin olive oil

1 teaspoon salt

1 teaspoon minced fresh thyme

1 teaspoon minced fresh rosemary

1 teaspoon minced fresh mint

Freshly ground pepper

24 chicken wings

• Combine the lemon zest and juice, olive oil, salt, herbs, and pepper to taste in a large bowl and whisk to blend. Add the chicken wings and toss to coat. Cover and marinate at room temperature for 1 hour, or refrigerate for at least 2 hours or as long as overnight. Return to room temperature if refrigerated.

• Preheat a grill or broiler. Drain the chicken wings, discarding the marinade. Grill, turning occasionally, until golden brown, 6 to 8 minutes. Arrange on a platter and serve warm. *Serves 8*

grilled scallops
wrapped in pancetta

This sweet marinade balances beautifully with the saltiness of the pancetta. For variety, substitute half of the scallops with shelled and deveined shrimp; the cooking time will be about the same, or until the shrimp are evenly pink.

¼ cup soy sauce

1 tablespoon grated orange zest

Juice of 1 orange

1 teaspoon grated fresh ginger

1 pound sea scallops, rinsed

8 slices pancetta or bacon, cut into strips about 1 by 3 inches

Olive oil for brushing

• Combine the soy sauce, orange zest and juice, and ginger in a bowl. Add the scallops and toss to coat. Cover and refrigerate for at least 30 minutes.

• Soak 16 bamboo skewers in water for 30 minutes.

• Preheat a grill or broiler. Wrap each scallop around the edges with a strip of pancetta and thread the skewer through the equator of the scallop and pancetta. Lightly brush with olive oil and grill, turning once or twice, until the pancetta is crisp, 6 to 8 minutes. Arrange on a platter and serve warm. *Serves 8*

grilled portobello mushrooms
with crumbled stilton

My preferred mushrooms for this dish are porcini, but they can be difficult to find. Portobello mushrooms are a good substitute. Use a grill basket to make it easier to turn the skewers.

4 portobello mushrooms, stemmed

½ cup extra-virgin olive oil

2 cloves garlic, minced

1 tablespoon minced fresh rosemary

4 ounces Stilton cheese

• Preheat a grill or broiler. With a grapefruit spoon or melon ball scoop, remove the gills from the underside of the mushrooms and cut the caps into ¼-inch-thick slices.

• Combine the olive oil, garlic, and rosemary in a medium bowl. Add the mushroom slices and toss to coat well. Grill, turning once, until lightly browned, 4 to 6 minutes. While still warm, arrange on a platter, crumble the cheese on top, and serve. *Serves 8*

stuffed & rolled

I remember my mother's stuffed celery appetizers from the '50s. Celery stalks filled with cream cheese or peanut butter . . . ah, things were much simpler back then! The recipes in this chapter are a bit more demanding on your time, but the flavors are equally rewarding. Most can be assembled in advance and cooked or finished at the last minute. When preparing rolled or stuffed items in advance, place them on a baking sheet lined with parchment paper so they can be moved easily later. Cover them tightly with plastic wrap and refrigerate. If your guests are fun-loving and like to cook, have them help assemble some of the dishes. Everyone ends up in the kitchen anyway, so why not put them to work?

fried spring rolls
with peanut dipping sauce

For a summer party, serve the spring rolls without frying.

peanut dipping sauce

$^1/_2$ cup canned coconut milk

$^1/_2$ cup smooth peanut butter

1 green onion, finely chopped, including 2 inches green parts

1 lemongrass stalk (white part only), peeled and minced

Juice of $^1/_2$ lime

2 cloves garlic, minced

1 tablespoon soy sauce

1 teaspoon curry powder

1 teaspoon ground coriander

$^1/_2$ teaspoon ground cumin

About 1 teaspoon chili paste

8 ounces rice noodles (cellophane noodles), soaked in hot water for 15 minutes

3 tablespoons peanut oil, plus more for deep-frying

1 garlic clove, minced

$^1/_2$ teaspoon toasted sesame oil

8 ounces Chinese broccoli (gai lan), coarsely chopped

1 carrot, peeled and shredded

$^1/_2$ cup mung bean sprouts

24 (6-inch) round rice papers

About 50 fresh mint leaves, plus more for garnish

About 50 fresh cilantro sprigs, plus more for garnish

24 butter lettuce leaves for serving

continued next page

fried spring rolls
(continued)

• For the peanut dipping sauce: Combine all the ingredients except the chili paste in a small saucepan. Cook over medium heat for 3 to 5 minutes, stirring constantly, until blended. Place in blender and puree until smooth, thinning with water if necessary. Add the chili paste to taste. *Makes about 1¼ cups*

• Drain the noodles, cut them into 2-inch lengths, and set aside.

• Heat the 3 tablespoons peanut oil in a wok or large, heavy sauté pan over medium-high heat. Add the garlic and cook until golden, about 3 minutes. Add the sesame oil, then the broccoli and carrot; stir-fry until softened, 4 to 6 minutes. Add the noodles and stir-fry until heated through, 2 to 3 minutes. Add the bean sprouts and set aside to cool.

• Soak the rice papers, one at a time, in tepid water until softened, 1 to 2 minutes. Drain and place 1 heaping tablespoon filling in the center of a paper and top with 1 or 2 mint leaves and cilantro sprigs. Fold from the bottom once, then fold in the sides and roll into a cylinder.

• Add 2 inches oil to a Dutch oven or deep fryer and bring to 365°F over medium-high heat. Add the rolls in batches of 2 or 3 and cook until golden, 4 to 5 minutes, turning occasionally with tongs to cook evenly. Using tongs, transfer each roll to paper towels to drain, and transfer to a low oven to keep warm until all the rolls are fried.

• Line a platter with the lettuce leaves, place a roll in each leaf, and garnish with the remaining mint and cilantro sprigs. Serve the peanut sauce alongside for dipping. *Makes 24 rolls*

grilled eggplant rolls
stuffed with herbed ricotta

If the slender Japanese eggplants are not available, a regular globe eggplant will work. Cut it into lengthwise slices about 2 inches wide, sprinkle with salt on both sides, and let drain for 30 minutes on a wire rack. Rinse, pat dry, and proceed to grill.

4 Japanese eggplants, cut lengthwise into ¼-inch-thick slices

Extra-virgin olive oil for brushing, plus 3 tablespoons

1 cup ricotta cheese

2 cloves garlic, minced

1 tablespoon minced fresh basil, plus 1 tablespoon finely shredded basil

Salt and freshly ground pepper

• Preheat a grill or broiler. Brush the eggplant lightly with olive oil. Grill or broil the eggplant on both sides until lightly browned, about 4 to 6 minutes. Remove from the heat and set aside to cool.

• Combine the ricotta cheese, garlic, and minced basil in a small bowl. Stir to blend and season with salt and pepper to taste.

• Spread a thin layer of the ricotta mixture on each slice of eggplant. Roll each slice lengthwise into a tight roll and secure with a toothpick. Place, seam side down, on a tray. Cover and refrigerate for at least 1 hour or as long as overnight. Garnish with the shredded basil and serve. *Serves 8*

tortilla rolls

This is a wonderful, festive do-ahead appetizer. Make the filling and the salsa up to a day ahead and assemble the tortillas just before serving. Have a bowl of chips nearby, as the salsa will be very popular!

corn and black bean salsa

1 (13-ounce) can black beans, drained and rinsed

3 tablespoons extra-virgin olive oil

1/2 cup thinly sliced green onions (including 1 inch of green parts)

1 red bell pepper, seeded, deribbed, and diced

2 cloves garlic, minced

1 jalapeño chili, seeded and minced

1 cup fresh or frozen corn kernels

1 teaspoon ground cumin

1/4 cup fresh cilantro leaves, minced

Salt and freshly ground pepper

1 pound spinach, stemmed, steamed for 3 minutes, and squeezed dry

8 ounces cream cheese

1 (4-ounce) can peeled green chilies, drained

1/4 cup finely chopped green onion

8 large flour tortillas

• For the salsa: Put the beans in a medium bowl and toss with the olive oil. Add the green onions, bell pepper, garlic, jalapeño, and corn; toss to blend. Season with cumin, cilantro, and salt and pepper to taste.

• Combine the spinach, cream cheese, and chilies in a food processor and pulse to a smooth consistency. Stir in the green onion.

• Spread about 2 heaping tablespoons cream cheese mixture onto each tortilla and roll up. Cut crosswise into 1-inch-thick diagonal slices and arrange on a platter. Put a small spoonful of salsa on top of each slice and serve. *Serves 8*

stuffed grape leaves
with dilled yogurt

If you don't have access to fresh grape leaves, substitute a 12-ounce jar of brined grape leaves, rinsed well, then blanched for 10 seconds.

3 dozen fresh young grape leaves, stemmed

4 tablespoons olive oil

1/2 cup finely chopped onion

1 bunch green onions, finely chopped (including 1 inch of green part)

1 cup long-grain white rice

2 cups chicken stock (page 104)

Juice of 2 lemons

1/4 cup minced fresh flat-leaf parsley

2 teaspoons minced fresh mint

2 tablespoons pine nuts

1/4 cup dried currants

1/4 teaspoon salt

Freshly ground pepper

1 cup Greek yogurt (see note)

2 tablespoons minced fresh dill

1 lemon, cut into wedges

• Blanch the grape leaves in boiling water for 15 seconds. Remove and pat dry. Spread out on a work surface, shiny side down.

• Heat 2 tablespoons of the olive oil in a large skillet over medium heat. Sauté the onion and green onions until softened, about 3 minutes. Add the rice and stir to coat with oil. Add the chicken stock and bring to a boil. Reduce to a simmer and cook until the liquid is absorbed, 20 to 25 minutes.

• Remove from the heat and stir in half of the lemon juice and all of the parsley, mint, pine nuts, and currants. Season with salt and pepper to taste.

• Place a heaping teaspoon of filling at the base of one of the grape leaves. Roll up from the bottom one turn, then fold in the sides and continue to roll toward the point of the leaf. Repeat with the remaining filling and leaves. Arrange the stuffed leaves snugly in a single layer in a large nonstick skillet. Sprinkle with 1 tablespoon of the olive oil and 3 tablespoons of the remaining lemon juice. Add water just to cover the stuffed leaves. Cover with a plate that just fits in the pan to weight the leaves. Simmer for 35 minutes, adding water if necessary. Remove from the heat and let cool.

• For the yogurt: In a small bowl, combine the yogurt and dill; stir to blend.

• Drain the rolls and arrange them on a platter. Drizzle with the remaining 1 tablespoon olive oil and remaining lemon juice. Serve at room temperature, with the dilled yogurt and lemon wedges. *Serves 8*

Note: If you don't have access to Greek yogurt, place 2 cups whole-milk yogurt in a sieve lined with cheesecloth; set the sieve over a bowl and let the yogurt drain in the refrigerator overnight.

egetable samosas

These can be made ahead and frozen, then baked without defrosting. Baba Ghanoush (page 20) makes a fantastic accompaniment.

2 potatoes, peeled and cut into 2-inch pieces

1 teaspoon curry powder

6 tablespoons extra-virgin olive oil

1/2 cup chopped onion

1 carrot, peeled and shredded

1/2 cup fresh or frozen green peas

3 tablespoons minced fresh cilantro

Salt and freshly ground pepper

2 sheets frozen puff pastry, thawed

1 egg beaten with 1 tablespoon water for egg wash

2 teaspoons caraway seeds

• Put the potatoes in a small saucepan with cold water to cover; bring to a boil, then cook at a brisk simmer until tender, 20 to 25 minutes. Mash with a fork, blending in the curry powder and 3 tablespoons of the oil. Set aside.

• Heat the remaining 3 tablespoons oil in a small sauté pan over medium heat and sauté the onion until softened, about 3 minutes. Add the carrot and sauté until softened, 3 to 4 minutes. Add to the mashed potatoes. Stir in the peas and cilantro. Season with salt and pepper to taste.

• Roll each puff pastry sheet on a lightly floured work surface to thin slightly. Cut out rounds with a 3-inch scallop-edged biscuit cutter. Place 1 teaspoonful of the potato filling in the center of each round. Brush the edges with the egg wash, fold in half, and press the edges together to seal tightly.

• Preheat the oven to 400°F. Oil a baking sheet or line it with parchment paper.

• Place the samosas on the prepared pan and brush with the remaining egg wash. Sprinkle with caraway seeds and refrigerate for at least 30 minutes or as long as overnight. Bake until golden brown, 15 to 18 minutes. Serve hot or keep warm in a low oven until ready to serve. Arrange on a platter and serve warm. *Serves 8*

stuffed cabbage rolls

This dish can be prepared ahead of time and even frozen until ready to bake and serve. Use a decorative oven-to-table casserole.

1 head green cabbage, cored

¼ cup extra-virgin olive oil

½ cup chopped onion

2 cloves garlic, minced

½ cup broccoli florets

½ cup shredded beet

½ cup shredded turnip

1½ cups chicken stock (page 104)

¾ cup long-grain white rice

¼ cup minced fresh flat-leaf parsley

¼ cup raisins

¼ cup tomato sauce

5 tablespoons fresh lemon juice

¼ teaspoon ground ginger

¼ teaspoon ground coriander

¼ teaspoon ground cinnamon

Salt and freshly ground pepper

2 cups tomato puree

3 tablespoons brown sugar

• Remove the tough outer leaves of the cabbage. Place the cabbage head in a pot and add boiling water to cover.

Cook over medium heat until the leaves begin to separate, 5 to 7 minutes. As they separate from the head, remove then with tongs and set aside until all of the leaves have been removed. Return the leaves to the water and cook until they become pliable, 3 to 4 minutes. Immerse immediately in ice water to stop the cooking, then drain and set aside.

• For the filling: Heat the oil in a medium saucepan over medium heat and sauté the onion and garlic until lightly golden, about 5 minutes. Add the broccoli, beet, and turnip and sauté for 1 minute, stirring. Stir in the chicken stock and then the rice. Cover and simmer for 30 minutes, or until the liquid is absorbed.

• Add the parsley, raisins, tomato sauce, 2 tablespoons of the lemon juice, the ginger, coriander, and cinnamon. Add salt and pepper to taste and mix well. Set aside.

• Trim the heavy rib off the base of each cabbage leaf. With a sharp knife, cut each leaf into a rough rectangle about 3 by 5 inches. Place a heaping tablespoon of the filling in the center. Roll the leaf once around the mixture, then fold in the sides and roll up completely. Secure the rolls with toothpicks. Place the rolls on a lightly oiled baking sheet and set aside.

• For the sauce: Combine the tomato puree, brown sugar, and the remaining 3 tablespoons lemon juice in a medium nonreactive saucepan. Bring to a simmer and cook for 10 minutes.

• Preheat the oven to 350°F. Pour over the cabbage rolls and bake for 30 minutes. Serve warm. *Serves 8*

crispy parmigiano shells

This appetizer comes with an edible dish. Other fillings can be used for the shells, such as a rice salad, julienned roasted peppers, or grilled chicken strips.

3 cups (12 ounces) shredded

   Parmigiano-Reggiano cheese

2 cups mixed greens

½ cup radish sprouts (daikon)

⅓ cup minced fresh basil

1 tablespoon balsamic vinegar

3 tablespoons extra-virgin olive oil

Salt and freshly ground pepper

• Preheat the oven to 375°F. Oil a baking sheet or line it with parchment paper. Lightly oil 8 cups of a muffin pan.

• Spread the cheese evenly on the prepared baking sheet, creating a 6-by-12-inch rectangle. Bake until cheese has melted into one solid piece, about 5 minutes. Remove from the oven and, working quickly, cut the cheese into eight 3-inch squares and return to the oven until golden, 4 to 6 minutes. Remove from the oven and quickly press a warm square into each of the prepared muffin cups. Let cool.

• Just before serving, toss the greens, sprouts, and basil together in a large bowl. Drizzle with the balsamic vinegar and olive oil and toss to coat well. Season with salt and pepper to taste and divide among the Parmigiano-Reggiano cups. Arrange on a platter and serve at once.

Serves 8

provençal tomato-basil tartlets

Served with a glass of chilled sparkling white or rosé wine, this is an elegant and filling summer starter.

1 package active dry yeast

¼ cup sugar

1 cup warm (105° to 115°F) milk

8 tablespoons extra-virgin olive oil

1 egg, beaten

4½ cups unbleached all-purpose flour

½ teaspoon salt

½ cup chopped tomatoes

**1 tablespoon minced fresh basil, plus
   8 large leaves, cut into fine shreds**

Salt and freshly ground pepper

1 pint cherry tomatoes, halved

1 teaspoon minced fresh thyme

1 teaspoon sugar

• Stir the yeast and sugar into the milk until dissolved. Let stand for 5 minutes, or until foamy. Add 4 tablespoons of the oil and the egg and set aside.

• Stir the flour and salt together in a large bowl. Add the yeast mixture and stir to make a smooth dough.

• Turn the dough onto a lightly floured work surface. Knead until smooth and elastic, 10 to 15 minutes. Place in an oiled bowl, turn to coat, and cover with a damp towel or plastic wrap. Let rise in a warm place until doubled in volume, about 1½ hours.

• Preheat the oven to 375°F. Lightly oil eight 1-cup ramekins.

• Punch the dough down and divide into 8 pieces. Form each piece into a ball. Let rest for 15 minutes, covered with a dry towel. Roll out each ball on a lightly floured board into a round about ⅛ inch thick. Place each in a prepared ramekin, with the edges hanging over the side.

baked brie
with apricots

This recipe is shamefully easy and sinfully delicious! A savory variation is to use pesto instead of jam and walnuts.

• Drain the chopped tomatoes and reserve the liquid. Combine the drained tomatoes, minced basil, and 3 tablespoons of the olive oil in a small bowl. Season with salt and pepper to taste. Divide evenly among the ramekins. Arrange the cherry tomatoes on top of the tarts and fold the edges over them, pleating as you go. Brush with the remaining 1 tablespoon olive oil and sprinkle with the thyme and sugar. Bake, basting once or twice with reserved tomato liquid, until the crust is lightly browned, about 20 minutes.

• Remove from the oven and let stand for 5 minutes. Sprinkle each of 8 salad plates with the shredded basil and place a tart on each to serve. *Serves 8*

1 pound Brie cheese

2 sheets frozen puff pastry, thawed

1 cup apricot jam

1/3 cup chopped walnuts

1 egg yolk beaten with 1 teaspoon water

• Line a baking sheet with parchment paper. Remove the outside rind from the Brie and cut the cheese into 16 equal-sized pieces. Set aside.

• Place the puff pastry sheets on a lightly floured work surface. With a sharp knife, cut each sheet into eight 3-inch squares. Place a piece of Brie, 1 tablespoonful jam, and 1 teaspoonful chopped walnuts in the center of each square. Brush the edges of each square with egg wash, fold into a triangle, and press to seal the edges. Place on the baking sheet and refrigerate until ready to serve.

• Preheat the oven to 425°F. Brush the pastry with the remaining egg wash and bake until golden brown, 10 to 12 minutes. Arrange on a tray and serve at once. *Serves 8*

prosciutto-wrapped asparagus

Prosciutto di Parma, the salty-sweet cured ham from Emilia-Romagna, pairs well with the asparagus, but you could also use shards of Parmigiano-Reggiano cheese.

16 spears asparagus, trimmed

Juice of 1 lemon

8 paper-thin slices prosciutto, chilled

• Peel the bottom stalk of each asparagus stalk lightly with a vegetable peeler. Prepare a pot of salted boiling water and add the lemon juice. Add the asparagus and cook until crisp-tender, 3 to 5 minutes, depending on the thickness of the asparagus. Drain and immediately immerse in ice water to stop the cooking. Drain and pat dry.

• With a very sharp knife, cut the chilled prosciutto into 1-inch-wide strips. Wrap 1 strip of the prosciutto around the middle of each asparagus spear. Arrange on a tray for passing.

Serves 8

stuffed zucchini blossoms

*Zucchini blossoms are common at farmers'
markets in the spring and summer. If available,
you can also use blossoms with baby zucchini
attached (see note).*

16 zucchini flowers

1/2 cup ricotta cheese

**1/2 cup (2 ounces) grated
   Parmigiano-Reggiano cheese**

1 teaspoon minced fresh thyme

**1 tablespoon minced fresh flat-leaf
   parsley**

1 teaspoon minced fresh mint

Salt and freshly ground pepper

• Preheat the oven to 400°F. Lightly oil a baking
sheet or line it with parchment paper.

• Gently rinse inside the zucchini flowers and
remove the stamens. Blanch the flowers in
boiling water until softened, about 5 seconds.
Drain and immediately immerse into ice water
to stop the cooking process. Drain at once and
dry on paper towels.

• Mix the ricotta, Parmigiano, and herbs together
in a small bowl until blended. Season with salt
and pepper to taste. Put the mixture in a pastry
bag fitted with a 1/2-inch tip. Fill each flower with
about 1 teaspoon of the cheese mixture. Twist
the ends slightly and place on the prepared pan.
Season with salt and pepper to taste.

• Cover tightly with aluminum foil and bake just
until heated through, about 10 minutes. Do not
overcook. Serve at once. *Serves 8*

Note: If your blossoms have baby zucchini
attached, cook as directed above, then use a
thin-bladed knife to cut the baby zucchini lengthwise into 2 or 3 thin slices, taking care not to
detach them from the flower. The slices can
then be fanned out for a lovely presentation.

roasted poblano chili

This is a slightly more labor-intensive recipe, but it's well worth the time! You can just stuff the chilies with your favorite cheese for a quicker appetizer.

8 poblano chilies, roasted and peeled (see page 105)

¼ cup olive oil

1 red onion, finely chopped

3 cloves garlic, minced

½ cup shellfish or vegetable stock (pages 104 and 105)

4 ounces shrimp, shelled, deveined, and coarsely chopped

2 tablespoons minced fresh cilantro

8 ounces fresh lump or pasteurized crabmeat

¾ cup fresh or frozen corn kernels

1 red bell pepper, seeded, deribbed, and diced

¼ cup shelled pumpkin seeds (pepitas), toasted (see page 105)

Salt and freshly ground pepper

• Make a slit down one side of each chili. Remove the seeds and veins and set aside.

• Heat the oil in a large sauté pan over medium heat and sauté the onion and garlic until softened, about 3 minutes. Add the stock and bring to a boil. Add the shrimp and cook until pink, about 3 minutes. Stir in the cilantro, crabmeat, corn, bell pepper, and pumpkin seeds; heat through. Season with salt and pepper to taste.

• Spoon about 2 tablespoons of the filling into each chili and arrange on a serving platter. Serve at room temperature. *Serves 8*

stuffed tomatoes

Prepare the filling and have the tomatoes stuffed and ready to bake just before your guests arrive. Out of the refrigerator and into the oven, they will be ready to serve in about 30 minutes.

6 small firm, ripe tomatoes

Salt for sprinkling

1/2 cup cooked rice

3 tablespoons minced fresh basil

2 tablespoons tomato paste

1 tablespoon extra-virgin olive oil

Salt and freshly ground pepper

3 tablespoons grated Parmigiano-Reggiano cheese

• Preheat the oven to 300°F. Lightly oil an 8-inch square baking dish.

• Cut off the top of each tomato. With a small spoon, carefully scoop out the insides, leaving a wall about 1/4 inch thick. Reserve the pulp. Salt the inside of the tomatoes and place them upside down on a wire rack to drain for 5 minutes.

• Puree the tomato pulp in a food processor or blender until smooth. Transfer to a bowl and add the rice, basil, tomato paste, and olive oil. Mix well and season with salt and pepper to taste.

• Divide the filling evenly among the tomatoes. Place in the prepared dish. Cover with aluminum foil, making sure the foil doesn't make contact with the tomatoes, and bake until the tomatoes are softened, 25 to 30 minutes. Uncover and top with the Parmigiano cheese. Brown under the broiler, about 3 inches from the heat source, until golden brown, 2 to 3 minutes. Arrange on a platter and serve at once. *Serves 8*

rice croquettes
filled with gorgonzola

Use a high-starch rice such as an Italian Arborio or Asian short-grain for this recipe so that the rice will be sticky.

2 cups cooked medium- or
   short-grain rice
2 ounces Gorgonzola Dolcelatte
   cheese, cut into ½-inch nuggets
3 large eggs, lightly beaten
1 cup fine dried bread crumbs
Canola oil for frying

• Form the rice into 16 small oval balls about 1½ inches in diameter, then tuck a nugget of the cheese into the center of each one. Press tightly to seal the cheese inside. Set aside on a plate.

• Pour the eggs into a shallow bowl; spread the bread crumbs in another shallow bowl. Dip each ball into the egg and then into the bread crumbs, coating well.

• Heat 1 inch oil in a large, heavy sauté pan over medium heat until shimmering. Working in batches so as not to crowd the pan, add the rice balls and fry, turning frequently, until golden brown, 3 to 4 minutes.

• Using a slotted spoon, transfer to paper towels to drain. Keep warm in a low oven while cooking the remaining balls. Arrange on a platter and serve at once. *Serves 8*

deviled quail eggs

Deviled eggs are a comfort food at some parties, and quail eggs are a sophisticated variation on this old favorite. Tobiko, or flying fish roe, is found in Asian specialty foods shops.

16 quail eggs

½ cup mayonnaise

Juice of 1 lemon

1 tablespoon Dijon mustard

1 teaspoon minced fresh flat-leaf parsley

1 tablespoon tiny (nonpareil) capers

Salt and freshly ground white pepper

4 teaspoons tobiko (flying fish roe)

• To keep the boiling eggs from cracking, fold a tea towel and fit it into the bottom of a heavy, medium saucepan. Add the quail eggs and tepid water to cover; bring to a boil over medium heat. Cook for 3 minutes, then remove with a slotted spoon and peel under cold running water. Set aside and let cool completely.

• Peel the eggs, then, using a very sharp thin-bladed knife, cut each in half lengthwise. Carefully remove the yolks and mash them in a bowl with a fork. Add the mayonnaise, lemon juice, and mustard. Stir in the parsley and capers and season with salt and pepper to taste.

• Spoon the mixture into a pastry bag fitted with a small star tip. Pipe into the egg white halves and garnish with the roe. Refrigerate for at least 30 minutes or as long as overnight. Arrange on a tray and serve. *Serves 8*

stuffed baby potatoes
with mushroom puree & creme fraîche

This mushroom puree is also a great filling in blanched and scooped-out baby turnips or baby summer squash.

2 tablespoons dried porcini

¼ cup warm water

8 ounces baby potatoes, scrubbed

2 tablespoons olive oil

2 shallots, minced

1 clove garlic, minced

1 pound white mushrooms, finely chopped

1 teaspoon minced fresh flat-leaf parsley

½ teaspoon minced fresh thyme

Pinch of salt

Freshly ground pepper

¼ cup crème fraîche or sour cream

1 bunch chives, minced

• Soak the porcini in the water in a small bowl for 30 minutes. Drain the porcini, straining and reserving the liquid. Chop the porcini and set aside.

• Prepare a pot of salted boiling water. Add the potatoes and cook until just tender when pierced with a knife, about 3 minutes. Immerse immediately in ice water to stop the cooking. Drain well and let cool. Cut the potatoes in half and scoop out a small hole in each half with a melon baller.

• Heat the oil in a medium skillet over medium heat and sauté the shallots and garlic until softened, about 3 minutes. Add the mushrooms, the reserved porcini liquid, and the porcini and cook until the liquid has evaporated, about 5 minutes. Add the parsley, thyme, salt, and pepper to taste. Remove from the pan and puree in a food processor until smooth.

• With a small spoon fill each hollowed-out potato with a dollop of crème fraîche. Top with a little of the mushroom puree and sprinkle with the chives. Arrange on a platter and serve at once. *Serves 8*

b'stilla

Your guests will treasure the sweet and savory flavors of this satisfying dish. It can be assembled ahead of time and baked at the last moment, filling your house with spicy aromas.

2 cups chicken stock (page 104)

1 pound skinless, boneless chicken
  breasts

1 onion, finely chopped

1/2 cup white or cremini mushrooms,
  coarsely chopped

2 tablespoons minced fresh
  flat-leaf parsley

Pinch of saffron threads

3 large eggs, lightly beaten

1/2 cup almonds, toasted
  (see page 105) and ground

1 tablespoon granulated sugar

1/2 teaspoon ground cinnamon

1/4 teaspoon ground ginger

1/4 teaspoon ground coriander

1 (8-ounce) package thawed
  frozen phyllo dough

3 tablespoons extra-virgin olive oil

1/4 cup confectioners' sugar

1 tablespoon ground cinnamon

- Lightly oil 12 nonstick muffin cups.

- Bring the chicken stock to a boil in a large pot. Add the chicken breasts, onion, mushrooms, parsley, and saffron. Lower the heat to a simmer and cook until chicken is tender, about 20 minutes. Remove the chicken and let cool. Continue to simmer the vegetables and stock; whisk in the eggs (they will scramble) and cook until creamy, about 10 minutes. Drain, reserving the egg mixture and the cooking liquid separately. Put the egg in a small bowl with ½ cup of the reserved cooking liquid and set aside.

- Cut the cooled chicken into small cubes and set aside. Combine the almonds, granulated sugar, cinnamon, ginger, and coriander in a small bowl and stir to blend; set aside.

- Cut the phyllo into twelve 4-inch squares. Brush one piece lightly with oil. Repeat with 3 more pieces, stacking each one with the corners slightly off center. Place in a muffin cup, pressing the bottom carefully down. Repeat to make the remaining cups.

- Preheat the oven to 400°F. Fill with a spoonful of the egg, a layer of chicken, and a sprinkle of the almond mixture. Fold the overhanging phyllo corners over the top, brush with a little more oil, and bake until golden brown, about 15 minutes.

- Transfer to a warmed platter to serve. Dust with the confectioners' sugar and cinnamon and serve immediately. *Makes 12 appetizers*

plated & sauced

Appetizers can also be served as the first course of a sit-down meal. All of the recipes in this chapter are suitable for serving at the table or as part of a buffet. Presentation is important for a seated meal. Make the emphasis the plate itself and the way the food is arranged and presented. Use your imagination to create interesting garnishes such as deep-fried sage leaves, sprigs of fresh herbs, or edible flower petals. Think of unique ways of saucing the plates; for example, serve a tiny pitcher on each plate, or squirt geometric designs with a squeeze bottle. Finally, when serving warm appetizers, warm the plates before adding the food. And, conversely, chill the plates for cold dishes.

lemon chicken escabeche

Escabeche is a Spanish dish of poached or fried fish in a vinegar- or citrus-based marinade. This Mexican version uses chicken and gives it a Latin flair. Be sure the chicken is completely cooled before you dice it, or it will shred.

4 lemons, halved crosswise

2 cloves garlic

1 cup fresh cilantro leaves

1/3 cup pine nuts

3 tablespoons extra-virgin olive oil

1 cup chicken stock (page 104)

1 whole skinless, boneless
 chicken breast

1 red bell pepper, seeded,
 deribbed, and diced

3/4 cup fresh or frozen corn kernels

1/4 cup diced jicama

Salt and freshly ground pepper

• Scoop the pulp from the lemon halves with a grapefruit spoon or teaspoon, reserving the pulp and juice. Strain the juice and set aside. Cut a small slice from the bottom of each lemon half so that it will stand upright.

• Make a cilantro pesto: With the food processor running, drop in the garlic. Add the cilantro leaves, pine nuts, reserved lemon juice, and olive oil. Process to a smooth paste and set aside.

• Bring the chicken stock to a boil. Add the chicken breast and lower the heat to a simmer. Cook until opaque throughout, about 20 minutes. Remove from the stock and let cool (reserve the stock for another use).

• Dice the cooled chicken and put it in a bowl. Add the bell pepper, corn, jicama, and cilantro pesto and toss to mix well. Season with salt and pepper to taste. Cover and refrigerate for at least 1 hour or as long as overnight.

• Place a lemon half on each plate. Spoon the chicken mixture into the lemon halves and serve.
Serves 8

mini salmon cakes

These mini salmon cakes make a light and flavorful appetizer, or they can be served as a small lunch entrée alongside a green salad.

1 pound salmon fillet, skin and pin bones removed

3 tablespoons extra-virgin olive oil

1 red onion, finely diced

1 red bell pepper, seeded, deribbed, and diced

1 tablespoon minced garlic

¼ cup minced fresh cilantro

½ cup dried bread crumbs

½ cup sour cream

Salt and freshly ground white pepper

1 teaspoon grated lemon zest

1 teaspoon minced fresh dill

• Using a very sharp knife, chop the salmon until it resembles the texture of ground meat.

• Heat 1 tablespoon of the olive oil in a medium sauté pan over medium heat and sauté the onion, bell pepper, and garlic until softened, 2 to 3 minutes. Remove from the heat and let cool. Add to the chopped salmon and mix well. Stir in

the cilantro, 2 tablespoons of the bread crumbs, and ¼ cup of the sour cream. Season with salt and pepper to taste.

• Put the remaining bread crumbs in a large, shallow dish. Form the salmon mixture into 16 patties, each about 2 inches in diameter and ½ inch thick. Coat each patty in the bread crumbs and place on a platter. Cover with plastic wrap and refrigerate for 1 hour or as long as overnight.

• Pour 1 inch of oil in a large, heavy sauté pan and heat to 375°F over medium heat. Add half of the salmon cakes and cook until browned, 2 to 3 minutes per side. Keep warm in a low oven while cooking the remaining cakes.

• Combine the remaining ¼ cup sour cream, the lemon zest, and dill in small bowl. Stir to blend. Place 2 salmon cakes on each of 8 warmed salad plates. Top each cake with a dollop of the sour cream mixture and serve warm. *Serves 8*

lamb fritters
with curry sauce

This is a hearty and very flavorful appetizer that can also double as a main course.

curry sauce

3 tablespoons canola oil

2 onions, sliced

1 carrot, peeled and shredded

2 cloves garlic, minced

2 cups canned coconut milk

2 tablespoons curry powder

Salt

lamb fritters

3 tablespoons olive oil

3 leeks, white part only, chopped

1 clove garlic, minced

1/2 cup all-purpose flour

1 1/2 pounds ground lamb

3 large egg yolks, beaten

3/4 cup dried bread crumbs

Salt and freshly ground pepper

Extra-virgin olive oil for frying

• Make the curry sauce: Heat the oil in a large saucepan over medium heat and sauté the onions until softened, about 3 minutes. Add the carrot and garlic and cook until softened, 2 to 3 minutes. Stir in the coconut milk and curry powder and bring to a boil. Remove from the heat and season with salt to taste. Keep warm until ready to serve. *Makes 3 cups*

• Make the fritters: Heat the olive oil in a medium sauté pan over medium heat and sauté the leeks and garlic until softened, 2 to 3 minutes. Remove from the heat and set aside.

• Spread the flour in a shallow bowl. Combine the leek mixture, lamb, and eggs in a large bowl; mix well. Stir in the bread crumbs and salt and pepper to taste. The mixture should be moist.

continued next page

lamb fritters
(continued)

• Shape into 16 patties about 3 inches in diameter. Lightly dredge the patties in the flour and shake to remove the excess flour. Cook now, or cover and refrigerate for up to 3 hours.

• Heat the oil in a large sauté pan over medium-high heat and cook the patties, turning as needed, until browned, 4 to 5 minutes. Drain on paper towels. Serve now, or transfer to a baking sheet and keep warm in a low oven for up to 2 hours.

• To serve, place the patties on individual plates. Spoon the curry sauce over the patties and serve at once. *Serves 8*

chicken & apple pâté

With a glass of Chardonnay, this rich pâté is the perfect starter for an elegant sit-down meal. Serve on top of a bed of lightly dressed mixed greens.

3 tablespoons unsalted butter

**1 pound Granny Smith apples,
    peeled, cored, and diced**

1 large onion, diced

2 pounds coarsely ground chicken

4 large eggs

3/4 cup dried bread crumbs

1/3 cup dried currants

**1/3 cup dried sweet or tart cherries
    soaked in 2/3 cup Marsala for
    30 minutes**

**3 tablespoons salt-cured capers,
    rinsed and drained**

2 teaspoons dried thyme, crumbled

1 teaspoon grated lemon zest

1 tablespoon fresh lemon juice

Salt and freshly ground pepper

• Preheat the oven to 350°F. Lightly oil an 8-cup terrine or loaf pan.

• Melt the butter in a small sauté pan over medium heat and sauté the apples and onion until golden. Remove from the heat and let cool.

• Combine the apple mixture and all the remaining ingredients in a large bowl and mix well. Pack the mixture into the prepared terrine; smooth the top with a rubber spatula.

• Bake until the terrine is brown and pulling away from the sides of the terrine, 45 to 50 minutes. Remove from the oven and let cool completely on a wire rack, then slice and serve on individual plates at room temperature or chilled. *Serves 8*

italian ruby chard custard

This is a favorite with vegetarians and meat lovers alike. The ruby chard adds a lovely color, but you can also substitute Swiss chard or spinach.

¼ cup extra-virgin olive oil

1 red onion, chopped

2 pounds red Swiss chard, stemmed and cut into julienne

¾ cup milk

4 large eggs, lightly beaten

1 cup (4 ounces) grated Parmigiano-Reggiano cheese

⅛ teaspoon freshly grated nutmeg

Salt and freshly ground pepper

• Preheat the oven to 375°F. Lightly oil eight ½-cup ramekins and place on a baking sheet.

• Heat the olive oil in a large sauté pan over medium heat and sauté the onion until softened, about 3 minutes. Add the chard and cook until tender, 4 to 5 minutes.

• Combine the chard mixture and the milk in a blender or food processor and puree until smooth. Let cool.

• Whisk the eggs into the chard mixture. Stir in the cheese, nutmeg, and salt and pepper to taste. Divide among the prepared ramekins.

• Place the ramekins in a hot water bath and bake until a knife inserted in the center of a custard comes out clean, 30 to 35 minutes. Place each ramekin on a salad plate and serve warm. *Serves 8*

four-seasons frittata

The four seasons are represented by the vegetables in this dish. Try it with a drizzle of aged balsamic vinegar when serving.

1 potato, peeled, halved, and cut into ¼-inch-thick slices
1 bunch asparagus, trimmed and cut into 3-inch lengths
6 tablespoons olive oil
1 small onion, diced
1 cup sliced white mushrooms
8 large eggs, lightly beaten
1 tablespoon minced fresh flat-leaf parsley
1 red bell pepper, seeded, deribbed, and cut into ¼-inch-thick strips
¼ cup grated Parmesan
Salt and freshly ground pepper

• Prepare a pot of salted boiling water. Drop in the potato slices and cook until just tender, about 1 minute. Immerse immediately in ice water to stop the cooking. Drain well and set aside.

• In the same water, cook the asparagus until crisp-tender, 2 to 4 minutes, depending on thickness. Drain and immediately immerse in ice water to stop the cooking. Drain and set aside.

• Heat 3 tablespoons of the olive oil in a medium nonstick skillet over medium heat and sauté the onion until golden, about 5 minutes. Add the mushrooms and cook until they are softened and their liquid has evaporated, about 8 to 10 minutes. Using a slotted spoon, transfer the mixture to a bowl and set aside. Return the pan to the stove and heat the remaining olive oil over medium heat. Add the eggs and parsley and cook, pushing the edges back and letting the liquid run under. After 3 to 4 minutes, when the egg has just begun to set, arrange the potato slices, asparagus, mushrooms, and bell pepper in four quadrants on top of the eggs. Sprinkle evenly with the cheese and season with salt and pepper to taste. Remove from the heat and slide onto a cutting board.

• Cut into 8 wedges and serve hot on warmed plates or at room temperature. *Serves 8*

marinated mussels & clams

This dish is an exquisite opener for an all-seafood dinner. Discard any mussels or clams that don't open during cooking.

2 tablespoons olive oil, plus ⅓ cup

½ cup chopped onion

3 tablespoons minced fresh flat-leaf parsley

1 teaspoon minced fresh thyme

¾ cup dry red wine

16 mussels, debearded and scrubbed

16 clams, scrubbed

2 cups cooked long-grain white rice

2 tablespoons red wine vinegar

2 tablespoons capers, drained

2 tomatoes, peeled, seeded, and diced (see page 105)

Salt and freshly ground pepper

• Heat the 2 tablespoons olive oil in a large, heavy saucepan and sauté the onion until softened, about 3 minutes. Add 2 tablespoons of parsley, thyme, red wine, mussels, and clams. Cover and cook over high heat, shaking the pan occasionally, until all of the mussels and clams have opened, about 5 minutes. Remove mussels and clams and set aside. Add 1 cup of the cooked rice to the pot and cook until thickened, 10 to 15 minutes.

• While the rice mixture is cooking, remove the mussels and clams from their shells, reserving the shells. Place the mussel and clam meat in a bowl and add the ⅓ cup olive oil and the red wine vinegar. Let stand for 15 minutes. Add the capers, tomatoes, and remaining parsley to the rice mixture and season with salt and pepper to taste. Spoon some of the mixture into each pair of shells.

• Using a slotted spoon, place a piece of clam or mussel meat on top of the rice in each appropriate shell. Arrange 2 mussels and 2 clams on each plate and sprinkle with any leftover filling; serve immediately. *Serves 8*

champagne oysters

Fresh, briny oysters are a festive appetizer that will whet the appetites of your guests for a special meal to come. Serve them with the same Champagne used to make the sauce, and your guests will swoon! You will need coarse sea salt to make a bed for each bowl of oysters.

16 oysters in the shell

Coarse sea salt

3 tablespoons walnut oil

2 leeks, white part only, cut into julienne

1½ cups Champagne

3 shallots, thinly sliced

Salt and freshly ground white pepper

• Shuck the oysters, reserving as much liquor as possible. Set aside. Wash the shells, drain, and pat dry. Line 8 shallow soup bowls with coarse salt. Place 2 oyster shells in each bowl.

• Heat the oil in a small sauté pan over medium heat and sauté the leeks until softened, about 4 minutes. Divide the leeks among the oyster shells.

• Add the Champagne to the pan used to cook the leeks and stir over medium heat. Add the shallots, increase the heat to high, and cook to reduce the liquid by half. Add the oysters and the reserved oyster liquor for 30 seconds, just to warm the oysters. Season with salt and pepper to taste. Place an oyster on top of each leek-filled shell. Spoon the reduced pan liquid over the oysters and serve immediately. *Serves 8*

shrimp & herb salad

Crabmeat makes a lovely variation in place of the shrimp. Serve as a refreshing cold starter for an alfresco lunch or dinner.

¼ cup extra-virgin olive oil

1 pound large shrimp, shelled and deveined

1 tablespoon minced garlic

¼ cup dry white wine

¼ cup rice vinegar

2 tablespoons minced fresh ginger

½ cup safflower oil

Salt and freshly ground pepper

2 cups assorted sprouts: fennel, daikon, sunflower

1 bunch watercress, stemmed

½ cup garlic chive flowers

• Heat the olive oil in a large sauté pan over medium heat and sauté the shrimp and garlic until the shrimp are evenly pink, about 3 minutes. Add the wine and cook 1 minute longer. Remove from the heat and let cool.

• For the vinaigrette: Combine the rice vinegar and ginger in a small bowl. Gradually whisk in the safflower oil. Season with salt and pepper to taste. Add the shrimp and toss to coat. Set aside and let stand for 15 minutes at room temperature or up to 1 hour in the refrigerator.

• Combine the sprouts, watercress, and garlic chive flowers in a large bowl. Toss to mix. Divide evenly among 8 chilled plates. Remove the shrimp from the vinaigrette with a slotted spoon and arrange on the salads. Drizzle the vinaigrette over the salads and serve at once.

Serves 8

orange-broccoli salad

Tangy Asian flavors brighten up broccoli for an appetizing starter or side dish.

½ teaspoon Szechuan peppercorns

¼ teaspoon red pepper flakes

¼ cup rice vinegar

Juice of 1 orange

2 tablespoons toasted sesame oil

1 tablespoon honey

2 tablespoons dark soy sauce

1 pound broccoli, cut into florets

2 oranges

2 tablespoons peanut oil

1 sweet white onion, coarsely chopped

• For the dressing: Grind the Szechuan peppercorns and pepper flakes in a spice grinder or mortar. Heat a small dry skillet over medium heat and toast the pepper for 1 minute to release the flavors. Remove from the heat.

• Combine the vinegar, orange juice, and pepper mixture in a small bowl. Whisk in the sesame oil, honey, and soy sauce. Set aside.

• Prepare a large pot of salted boiling water. Drop in the broccoli and cook for about 1 minute, until crisp-tender. Immerse immediately in ice water to stop the cooking. Drain well and set aside.

• Cut off the top and bottom of the oranges down to the flesh. Stand each orange on end and cut off the peel down to the flesh with a large, sharp knife, removing as much of the white pith as possible. Cut vertically along both sides of each membranes to free the segments of orange. Put the segments in a medium bowl, adding any juice from the cutting board. Set aside.

• Heat the peanut oil in a medium sauté pan over medium heat and sauté the onion until just softened. Add the broccoli and cook just long enough to coat with oil and heat through. Remove from the heat and add the orange slices and their juices. Toss the broccoli with the dressing and serve on salad plates. *Serves 8*

roasted garlic & leek soufflé

Here is an elegant appetizer that is not a do-ahead recipe. You can, however, make the garlic puree ahead and finish the rest in the hour before serving.

4 heads garlic

½ cup olive oil

Salt and freshly ground pepper

¼ cup finely grated Parmigiano-Reggiano cheese for coating

4 tablespoons unsalted butter

2 tablespoons all-purpose flour

1 cup whole milk, heated

6 leeks, white part only, cut into julienne

1 tablespoon fresh lemon juice

3 large eggs, separated

• For the roasted garlic puree: Preheat the oven to 300°F. Lightly oil a small roasting pan. Score the skin around the middle of each head of garlic without cutting into the cloves, Remove the top half of the papery skin, exposing the cloves. Place the garlic in the prepared pan and pour the olive oil over the heads. Season with salt and pepper to taste. Cover and bake for 1 hour. Uncover and bake, basting frequently, until the heads are very tender, 10 to 15 minutes more. Remove from the oven and let cool. Squeeze the cloves from the skin and mash with a fork to puree.

- Preheat the oven to 375°F. Butter eight 1-cup ramekins and dust the bottom and sides with cheese.

- Melt 2 tablespoons of the butter in a small saucepan over medium heat. Whisk in the flour and cook, whisking constantly, for about 3 minutes. Gradually whisk in the milk, bring the mixture to a boil, then reduce to a simmer and stir until thickened. Remove the sauce from the heat and set aside.

- Melt the remaining 2 tablespoons butter in a medium sauté pan and sauté the leeks until softened, about 5 minutes. Combine the leeks, sauce, garlic puree, and lemon juice in a food processor and process until smooth. With the machine running, add the egg yolks. Stir in salt and pepper to taste. Set aside.

- Beat the egg whites to stiff, glossy peaks in a large bowl. Stir one-fourth of the beaten whites into the leek mixture. Fold in the remaining whites.

- Divide evenly into the prepared dishes. Place the dishes in a roasting pan and add hot water to come halfway up the sides of the ramekins. Bake until puffed and lightly golden, about 20 minutes. Place each ramekin on a small plate and serve at once. *Serves 8*

basics

chicken stock

3 pounds chicken parts

1 carrot, peeled and cut into ¹/₂-inch pieces

1 stalk celery, cut into ¹/₂-inch pieces

1 onion, cut into ¹/₂-inch pieces

Bouquet garni: 1 parsley sprig, 1 bay leaf,
1 thyme sprig, and 4 or 5 peppercorns,
tied in a cheesecloth square

1 gallon water

Combine all of the ingredients in a nonreactive stockpot and bring to a boil. Lower the heat to a simmer and skim the foam from the top. Simmer, uncovered, for 2 hours, skimming occasionally. Remove from the heat and let cool. Strain and refrigerate the stock overnight. Remove the solidified fat from the top. Refrigerate the stock for up to 3 days or freeze for up to 3 months. *Makes 12 cups*

shellfish stock

2 tablespoons extra-virgin olive oil

¹/₂ onion, coarsely chopped

1 carrot, peeled and coarsely chopped

1 stalk celery, coarsely chopped

¹/₄ cup dry white wine

8 cups water

At least 3 cups shrimp and/or lobster shells

Bouquet garni: 1 parsley sprig, 1 bay leaf,
1 thyme sprig, and 4 or 5 peppercorns,
tied in a cheesecloth square

Heat the olive oil in a nonreactive stockpot over medium heat and sauté the onion, carrot, and celery until softened, 3 to 4 minutes. Add the wine, stirring to loosen the cooked bits from the bottom of the pan. Increase the heat to medium-high and cook to reduce the wine until almost completely evaporated.

Add the water, shells, and bouquet garni. Bring to a boil, lower the heat to a simmer, and cook for at least 30 minutes or up to an hour. Strain the stock and discard the solids. Let cool, cover, and refrigerate for up to 2 days or freeze for up to 2 months. *Makes 6 cups*

vegetable stock

2 tablespoons extra-virgin olive oil

½ onion, coarsely chopped

1 carrot, peeled and coarsely chopped

1 stalk celery, coarsely chopped

¼ cup dry white wine

8 cups water

Bouquet garni: 1 parsley sprig, 1 bay leaf,
**   1 thyme sprig, and 4 or 5 peppercorns,**
**   tied in a cheesecloth square**

Heat the olive oil in a nonreactive stockpot over medium heat and sauté the onion, carrot, and celery until lightly browned, 5 to 8 minutes. Add the wine and stir to loosen the cooked bits from the bottom of the pan. Increase the heat to medium-high and cook to reduce the wine until almost completely evaporated. Add the water and the bouquet garni. Bring to a boil, lower the heat to a simmer, and cook for at least 45 minutes or up to 1 hour. Strain the stock and discard the solids. Let cool, cover, and refrigerate for up to 3 days or freeze for up to 3 months. *Makes 6 cups*

preparation tips

Toasting Nuts: Put the nuts on a baking sheet and toast in a preheated 350°F oven for 8 to 10 minutes, or until golden brown and aromatic. Pine nuts take less time, about 5 to 7 minutes.

Roasting and Peeling Peppers: Place whole peppers directly over a high flame. If you do not have a gas stovetop, use a grill or put the peppers on a baking sheet under your broiler. Turn the peppers frequently until blackened all over. Place them in a brown paper bag to steam and cool down. Peel the peppers by scraping the blackened skin off with a sharp knife. Remove the stem and seeds before cutting as directed in the recipe.

Peeling and Seeding Tomatoes: Cut out the core of each tomato. Drop the tomatoes in a pot of boiling water and blanch for 30 seconds; transfer immediately to ice water to stop the cooking and release the peels, which will slip off in your hands. To seed, cut the tomatoes in half and squeeze out the seeds.

equivalents

weights and measures

	liquid	dry	liquid	dry
1 teaspoon	⅓ tablespoon			5 grams
1 tablespoon	3 teaspoons			15 grams
2 tablespoons	⅛ cup	1 ounce	¼ deciliter (dL)	30 grams
4 tablespoons	¼ cup	2 ounces	½ dL	60 grams
5⅓ tablespoons	⅓ cup			75 grams
16 tablespoons	1 cup			200 grams
2 cups	1 pint	1 pound	½ liter	450 grams
2 pints (pt)	1 quart (4 cups)	32 ounces	1 liter	900 grams

dry ingredients

ounces	grams	grams	ounces
1	28.35	1	0.035
2	56.70	2	0.07
3	85.05	3	0.11
4	113.40	4	0.14
5	141.75	5	0.18
6	170.10	6	0.21
7	198.45	7	0.25
8	226.80	8	0.28
9	255.15	9	0.32
10	283.50	10	0.35

liquid ingredients

ounces	milliliters	milliliters	ounces
1	29.573	1	0.034
2	59.15	2	0.07
3	88.72	3	0.10
4	118.30	4	0.14
5	147.87	5	0.17
6	177.44	6	0.20
7	207.02	7	0.24
8	236.59	8	0.27
9	266.16	9	0.30
10	295.73	10	0.33

quarts	liters	liters	quarts
1	0.946	1	1.057
4	3.79	4	4.23

gallons	liters	liters	gallons
1	3.785	1	0.264

acknowledgments

This book evolves from a team effort, and I appreciate everyone's contribution: Jennifer Barry's gifted creative inspiration, publisher Kirsty Melville's continuing confidence, Lane Butler's editorial guidance, Joyce Oudkerk Pool's elegant photography, Pouké Halpern's inspired styling, and Carolyn Miller's precise editing.

Thanks, too, to my husband, Courtney, and my daughter, Alaia, for their love and their appetites. And in memory of my mother, who truly started me in the kitchen, I send a thank you from my heart.

sources

Ace Hardware
Tel: 866-290-5334
www.acehardware.com
Flexible stainless steel cable skewers

Crate & Barrel
(stores nationwide)
Catalog: 800-323-5461
www.crateandbarrel.com
Serving dishes, kitchen tools, skewers, and picks

Manicaretti
5332 College Avenue, No. 200
Oakland, CA 94618
Tel: 800-799-9830
www.manicaretti.com
Importer of artisanal Italian foods, such as pasta, olives, capers, vinegars, salt, anchovies, fennel pollen, dried herbs

Market Hall Foods
Tel: 888-952-4005
Fax: 510-652-4669
www.markethallfoods.com
A high-quality selection of international products

Niman Ranch
Tel: 866-808-0340
Fax: 510-808-0339
www.nimanranch.com
High-quality fresh and cured domestic meats

Rome Industries
Tel: 800-818-7603
www.romeindustries.com
Specialty skewers

Sur La Table
(stores nationwide)
Catalog: 800-243-0852
www.surlatable.com
Fine foods and serving dishes, kitchen tools, specialty skewers, and picks

Tool Wizard
Tel: 800-630-8665
www.toolwizard.com
Double-prong skewers, kebab forks, and seasoned skewers

Williams-Sonoma
(stores nationwide)
Catalog: 800-541-2233,
877-812-6235
www.williams-sonoma.com
Fine foods and serving dishes, kitchen tools, and specialty skewers

Learn to Cook in Italy:

Italian Food Artisans/Culinary Arts, Intl.
U.S. office: Tel: 805-963-7289
Fax: 805-456-0653
www.foodartisans.com
Wine and food workshops with the author in several regions of Italy; bed-and-breakfast at the author's farm in Montepulciano (Tuscany).

index

A

Apple
    and chicken pâté, 93
    slices, chicken liver crostini
        with, 18
Apricots, baked Brie with, 71
Artichokes, baby, with red pepper
    mayonnaise, 24–25
Arugula mini pizzas, prosciutto
    and, 33
Asparagus
    four-seasons frittata, 95
    prosciutto-wrapped, 72
Avocado-papaya salsa with
    quesadilla triangles, 26

B

Baba ghanoush with toasted pita
    triangles, 20
Baby artichokes with red pepper
    mayonnaise, 24–25
Baby potatoes, stuffed, with
    mushroom puree and creme
    fraîche, 81
Baby vegetables, grilled, 41
Baked Brie with apricots, 71
Beans
    black, and corn salsa, tortilla rolls
        with, 61
    white bean–rosemary crostini, 12
Bite-sized polenta squares with
    goat cheese and sun-dried
    tomatoes, 29
Bread. See also Crostini
    baba ghanoush with toasted pita
        triangles, 20
    heirloom tomato bruschetta, 17
    potato–red onion flat, 30–32

twists, spicy, pesto dip with,
    14–15
Brie, baked, with apricots, 71
Broccoli
    fried spring rolls, 56–58
    -orange salad, 100
    stuffed cabbage rolls, 66–67
Bruschetta, heirloom tomato, 17
B'stilla, 82–83

C

Cabbage rolls, stuffed, 66–67
Champagne oysters, 98
Chard custard, Italian ruby, 94
Cheese. See individual cheeses
Cherry tomato skewers,
    mozzarella, basil, and, 45
Chicken
    and apple pâté, 93
    b'stilla, 82–83
    escabeche, lemon, 86
    liver crostini with apple slices,
        18
    stock, 104
    wings, grilled lemon, 48
    wings, tea-smoked, 34
Chilies, roasted poblano, stuffed
    with shrimp and crab, 75
Cilantro–pine nut dipping sauce,
    scallops with, 35
Clams, marinated mussels and, 97
Corn and black bean salsa, tortilla
    rolls with, 61
Crab, roasted poblano chilies
    stuffed with shrimp and, 75
Creme fraîche, stuffed baby
    potatoes with mushroom puree
    and, 81

Crispy Parmigiano shells stuffed
    with mixed greens, 69
Croquettes, rice, filled with
    Gorgonzola, 78
Crostini
    chicken liver, with apple slices,
        18
    white bean–rosemary, 12
Curry sauce, lamb fritters with,
    91–92
Custard, Italian ruby chard, 94

D

Deviled quail eggs with capers
    and flying fish caviar, 79
Dilled yogurt, stuffed grape leaves
    with, 62–63
Dips
    baba ghanoush with toasted
        pita triangles, 20
    herbed goat cheese, 23
    pesto, with spicy bread twists,
        14–15

E

Eggplant
    baba ghanoush with toasted
        pita triangles, 20
    rolls, grilled, stuffed with herbed
        ricotta, 59
Eggs
    deviled quail, with capers and
        flying fish caviar, 79
    four-seasons frittata, 95
    roasted garlic and leek soufflé,
        102–3
Equivalents, 106
Escabeche, lemon chicken, 86

F

Fish
  mini salmon cakes, 89
  pepper-crusted tuna, onion, and bell pepper skewers, 40
Flat bread, potato–red onion, 30–32
Food safety, 7
Four-seasons frittata, 95
Fried spring rolls with peanut dipping sauce, 56–58
Frittata, four-seasons, 95
Fritters, lamb, with curry sauce, 91–92
Fruit, grilled fresh, 42

G

Garlic, roasted, and leek soufflé, 102–3
Goat cheese
  dip, herbed, with crudité, 23
  and sun-dried tomatoes, bite-sized polenta squares with, 29
Gorgonzola, rice croquettes filled with, 78
Grape leaves, stuffed, with dilled yogurt, 62–63
Greens, crispy Parmigiano shells stuffed with mixed, 69
Grilled baby vegetables, 41
Grilled eggplant rolls stuffed with herbed ricotta, 59
Grilled fresh fruit, 42
Grilled lemon chicken wings, 48
Grilled portobello mushrooms with crumbled Stilton, 62
Grilled scallops wrapped in pancetta, 51
Grilled shrimp skewers, 38

H

Heirloom tomato bruschetta, 17
Herbed goat cheese dip with crudité, 23
Herbed ricotta, grilled eggplant rolls stuffed with, 59

I

Italian ruby chard custard, 94

L

Lamb fritters with curry sauce, 91–92
Leek and roasted garlic soufflé, 102–3
Lemon chicken escabeche, 86
Lemon chicken wings, grilled, 48

M

Marinated mushrooms, 21
Marinated mussels and clams, 97
Mayonnaise, red pepper, baby artichokes with, 24–25
Meatballs, skewered Hawaiian sweet and sour, 46–47
Menus, thematic, 7–9
Mini salmon cakes, 89
Mozzarella, basil, and cherry tomato skewers, 45
Mushrooms
  marinated, 21
  portobello, grilled, with crumbled Stilton, 52
  puree and creme fraîche, stuffed baby potatoes with, 81
Mussels and clams, marinated, 97

N

Nuts, toasting, 105

O

Orange-broccoli salad, 100
Oysters, Champagne, 98

P

Pancetta, grilled scallops wrapped in, 51
Papaya
  -avocado salsa with quesadilla triangles, 26
  grilled fresh fruit, 42
Parmigiano shells, crispy, stuffed with mixed greens, 69
Party planning, 5–6
Pâté, chicken and apple, 93
Peanut dipping sauce, fried spring rolls with, 56–58
Peeling and seeding tomatoes, 105
Peppers
  bell, pepper-crusted tuna, and onion skewers, 40
  mayonnaise, red, 24–25
  poblano chilies, roasted, 75
  roasting and peeling, 105
Pesto dip with spicy bread twists, 14–15
Pineapple
  grilled fresh fruit, 42
  skewered Hawaiian sweet and sour meatballs, 46–47
Pizzas, prosciutto and arugula mini, 33
Poblano chilies, roasted, stuffed with shrimp and crab, 75
Polenta squares, bite-sized, with goat cheese and sun-dried tomatoes, 29
Portobello mushrooms, grilled, with crumbled Stilton, 52
Potatoes
  four-seasons frittata, 95
  –red onion flat bread, 30–32
  stuffed baby, with mushroom puree and creme fraîche, 81
  vegetable samosas, 64

Presentation, 6–7, 85
Prosciutto
    and arugula mini pizzas, 33
    -wrapped asparagus, 72
Provençal tomato-basil tartlets, 70

Q

Quail eggs, deviled, with capers
    and flying fish caviar, 79
Quesadilla triangles, papaya-
    avocado salsa with, 26

R

Red pepper mayonnaise, 24–25
Rice
    croquettes filled with
        Gorgonzola, 78
    stuffed cabbage rolls, 66–67
    stuffed grape leaves with dilled
        yogurt, 62–63
    stuffed tomatoes, 77
Ricotta, herbed, grilled eggplant
    rolls stuffed with, 59
Roasted garlic and leek soufflé,
    102–3
Roasted poblano chilies stuffed
    with shrimp and crab, 75
Roasting and peeling peppers, 105
Ruby chard custard, Italian, 94

S

Salads
    orange-broccoli, 100
    shrimp and herb, 99
Salmon cakes, mini, 89
Salsas
    corn and black bean, tortilla rolls
        with, 61
    papaya-avocado, with quesadilla
        triangles, 26
Samosas, vegetable, 64
Sauces. *See also* Salsas
    cilantro–pine nut dipping, 35

curry, lamb fritters with, 91–92
    peanut dipping, 56–58
    sweet and sour dipping, 34
Scallops
    with cilantro–pine nut dipping
        sauce, 35
    grilled, wrapped in pancetta, 51
Seeding tomatoes, peeling and, 105
Shellfish stock, 104
Shrimp
    and herb salad, 99
    roasted poblano chilies stuffed
        with crab and, 75
    shellfish stock, 104
    skewers, grilled, 38
Skewered Hawaiian sweet and
    sour meatballs, 46–47
Soufflé, roasted garlic and leek,
    102–3
Sources, 108
Spring rolls, fried, with peanut
    dipping sauce, 56–58
Stilton, crumbled, grilled portobello
    mushrooms with, 52
Stocks
    chicken, 104
    shellfish, 104
    vegetable, 105
Stuffed baby potatoes with
    mushroom puree and creme
    fraîche, 81
Stuffed cabbage rolls, 66–67
Stuffed grape leaves with dilled
    yogurt, 62–63
Stuffed tomatoes, 77
Stuffed zucchini blossoms, 74
Sweet and sour meatballs,
    skewered Hawaiian, 46–47

T

Tartlets, Provençal tomato-basil, 70
Tea-smoked chicken wings, 34

Toasting nuts, 105
Tomatoes
    -basil tartlets, Provençal, 70
    bruschetta, heirloom, 17
    cherry, mozzarella, and basil
        skewers, 45
    peeling and seeding, 105
    stuffed, 77
    sun-dried, bite-sized polenta
        squares with goat cheese
        and, 29
Tortillas
    papaya-avocado salsa with
        quesadilla triangles, 26
    rolls with corn and black bean
        salsa, 61
Tuna, pepper-crusted, onion, and
    bell pepper skewers, 40

V

Veal
    skewered Hawaiian sweet and
        sour meatballs, 46–47
Vegetables. *See also individual
    vegetables*
    grilled baby, 41
    herbed goat cheese dip with
        crudité, 23
    samosas, 64
    stock, 105
Vegetarian recipes, 9

W

White bean–rosemary crostini, 12

Y

Yogurt, dilled, stuffed grape leaves
    with, 62–63

Z

Zucchini blossoms, stuffed, 74